THE JOYFUL GARDENER

By AGNES ROTHERY
Author of A FITTING HABITATION, *etc.*

This enchanting book is written for every one who likes to read about gardens or look at gardens or work in gardens.

Its purpose, as the title implies, is not primarily to tell you what to do in your garden, but how to enjoy it, and to enjoy all gardens, fabulous and actual, famous and simple, stretching from one edge of the world to the other. While it contains a tremendous amount of curious and amusing information, it is written so pleasantly that the reader is hardly aware of the range of scholarship, botanical and literary, which gives it body.

It is a book for the lazy reader as well as for the hard-working expert: for the beginner, the optimist, the procrastinator, the decorator. It is delightful bedside reading and a perfect gift book. You will be charmed with its gaiety, humor and sentiment; and without realizing it you will find out a good many things about gardens, including poets and painters, poisoners and perfumers, saints, sinners, scientists, animals and garden clubs.

Agnes Rothery has been called the most graceful living American essayist. THE JOYFUL GARDENER is her happiest accomplishment since A FITTING HABITATION.

THE JOYFUL GARDENER

BOOKS BY AGNES ROTHERY

BIOGRAPHY

Family Album
A Fitting Habitation

JUVENILES

South American Roundabout
Washington Roundabout
Central American Roundabout
Scandinavian Roundabout
Maryland and Virginia Roundabout
Iceland Roundabout

NOVELS

The House by the Windmill
The High Altar
Into What Port?
Balm of Gilead

A PLAY

Miss Coolidge

THE

Joyful Gardener

BY AGNES ROTHERY

ILLUSTRATED BY LEE VITALE

Dodd, Mead & Company

NEW YORK

PRINTED IN THE UNITED STATES OF AMERICA
AMERICAN BOOK–STRATFORD PRESS, INC., NEW YORK
55

To My Sister Peggy

ACKNOWLEDGMENTS

Acknowledgment and thanks are due to the following authors, publishers, and copyright holders for permission to use passages of prose and poetry:

The Bodley Head Ltd. London (for Canada) and Dodd, Mead & Company: "They Are Not Long" and "To One in Bedlam" from *The Poems of Ernest Dowson;* "In the Mushroom Meadows" from *Gardens Overseas and Other Poems* by Thomas Walsh.

The Clarendon Press, Oxford: Poem by Andrew Marvell.

Dorothy Graham: Selections from *Chinese Gardens.*

The Macmillan Company: "A Duet" from *Collected Poems of T. Sturge Moore;* two verses from "Lavender" from *Collected Poems of Katherine Tynan;* and "Sweet Breeze" from *Collected Poems of T. E. Brown.*

Charles Scribner's Sons: Selections from *Father and Son* by Edmund Gosse.

Theodore T. Whitney: "A Violet" by Mrs. A. D. T. Whitney.

I also wish to thank *The Virginia Quarterly Review* and *House Beautiful Magazine* for their permission to reprint material which has appeared in their pages.

CONTENTS

THE JOYFUL GARDENER

Lord, when I look at lovely things which pass,
    Under old trees the shadow of young leaves
Dancing to please the wind along the grass.
    Or the gold stillness of the August sun on the August
        sheaves;
Can I believe there is a heavenlier world than this?
    And if there is
Will the strange heart of any everlasting thing
    Bring me these dreams that take my breath away?
They come at evening with the home-flying rooks and the
        scent of hay
    Over the fields. They come in Spring.

CHARLOTTE MEW

GARDENS IN A BASKET

Sweet-Shrub

CALYCANTHUS

I had just finished putting the flower garden in order for the winter. The last chrysanthemum was cut down, the compost was spread smoothly. "This is the way a garden should look," I thought, as I surveyed it, "without a weed; only a few rosettes of the perennials, and the clipped leaves of the iris, the columbine and stock still green above the brown surface."

Suddenly, and with violence, the gale I had been sniffing, and hoping might veer off, swept in from the east. It lashed the shrubs and tore the last withered leaves from the trees. Almost simultaneously a cold dark rain slanted down and as I dashed for the house I acknowledged the end of gardening for this year.

As I ran I could feel, rustling in my pocket, the envelopes into which I had slipped seeds from the pastel hollyhocks and some pods from the datura. I must put these with other envelopes in the box on the shelf with the garden catalogues, guides, diaries and calendar instructions. Above this shelf are several rows of garden books: volumes botanical, horticultural, sentimental, facetious; anthologies of garden poetry and flower lore. On the lowest shelf of all is a brown basket, its lid fastened so that the bookcase looks quite as tidy as the garden I have just finished putting in order.

This, actually, is not the case. I have been saving things in that basket for ages, so, although with its cover closed it gives the deception of neatness, it is an appalling hodgepodge.

This long end of the afternoon, with the longer evening to follow, is just the time to clean out the jumble, throw away the rubbish and file whatever is worth saving.

I sit down on the floor and pull the basket to my lap.

It is not the usual shape for a basket, for although it is woven of tan and yellow reed, its edges bound with a rattan-like black, it is oblong, with a lid fastened down by three loops along the back and with a larger loop and a peg on the cord in front, and it has a stout handle for easy carrying.

I bought it one summer in Martinique, when our accumulating possessions necessitated more room than our bags afforded. As a matter of fact, there were three matching cases made of three sizes, so that they fitted one inside the other and could be carried as a single piece of luggage.

They were all crammed, I remember, when we left Martinique.

The two smaller ones have disappeared. This third and largest is almost the size of a suitcase and now, as I draw the peg which serves as a latch and lift the lid, the pressed and crowded contents suddenly bulge and rise up like a wildly disheveled and tattered jack-in-the-box.

Clippings, notebooks, twists of paper containing seeds, cards with addresses of people and places and plants. A page from a magazine with pictures of gardening aprons and smocks; an advertisement of gardening tools; sketches of homemade cold frames and greenhouses. There is a small box with the silky white balls and thin stiff stems of cotton flowers from Finland, a handkerchief tied in a bunch with some crumbling brownish blossoms of sweetshrub from Sweden and another with twigs of dried thyme picked on the sandy uplands of Iceland. There are some tiny gourds from Mexico, a few delicately colored sea shells from Cartagena, a small flat gray stone, perfectly smooth and perfectly circular, picked up near King Arthur's castle at Tintagel. This glass ball, pockmarked by sand, had been detached from a fisherman's net and washed up on the beach at Yokohama. There is even an irregular lump of amber which my eye had caught glistening on the seaside near Palermo, and between two pieces of cardboard a frond of pressed and reddish seaweed from—where? It is not marked.

I have no idea where to begin. I uncrinkle a scrap of paper and see in my hasty jotting, "10 ounces of kerosene, 5 ounces of water, 1 ounce of flax soap." Yes, I remember now, the head gardener told me this recipe for an insecticide and I scratched it down as I stood in the damp warmth of his potting shed behind the gardens of the Empress Hotel in Victoria.

Here is a paragraph torn from a newspaper which falls in pieces when I unfold it, so that all I can make out is ". . . seeds and leaves of nasturtiums give a tangy fillip to a green salad." On the border of the menu from a hotel in Shanghai is my penciled scrawl, "Might try slices of raw turnip soaked in vinegar as a substitute for . . ." The menu is torn off at this point.

This has slipped out from a loose leaf notebook which seems quite filled with my handwriting. I open it at random and read, ". . . What boots it to wear out the soul with anxious thoughts? I want not wealth; I want not power; heaven is beyond my hopes. Then let me stroll through the bright hours as they pass, in my garden among my flowers . . . Thus will I work out my allotted space, content with appointments of Fate, my spirit free from care." (From the "Peach Blossom Fountain" by Lao Ch'ien. A.D. 365–427.)

I am puzzled. Why should raw turnips sliced and soaked in vinegar be kept with these notes on Chinese philosophers? I remember now. One winter long ago I read all the books I could find about Chinese gardens. Sometime, I thought, I would like to write something about them.

I must have moved inadvertently for, without warning, the basket tips, gapes wide and pours its flotsam and jetsam into my lap, over my knees, in a great deluge that floods the floor.

Like spring riches tumbling out from the cornucopia of nature, the scraps of paper, the seeds, the pebbles and shells and dried flower heads and pressed seaweed, pile in upturned layers, whisper into silence, as dormant soil, overturned by the plough, rises, is opened to the light and gradually settles down.

It will be several months before the fecundity of early spring is made manifest. It will be months before I can merge my energy with the dynamic energy of growing things. My actual garden is quiescent, but all around me spreads another and potential one— the garden of imagination and reflection.

All spring, all summer, all fall, we can see our garden with our eyes, feel it with our hands, breathe in its almost palpable fragrance. Swept by the final autumn gale, with winter on its wings, the foam of color, the billows of exquisite form which had broken into their ultimate crest are covered beneath the heavy gray waves of winter. The gardener's passion may be deflected, but it surges until it finds another outlet. It cannot relinquish its urgent necessity to bring forth, to share in the miracle of creation. When the garden outdoors is sealed away, one cultivates the garden of the mind.

I sat for a long time with my hands lying on the opened basket from Martinique.

Then I thought, "I will write a book about gardens."

When daisies go, shall winter time
Silver the simple grass with rime;
Autumnal frosts enchant the pool
And make the cart-ruts beautiful;
And when snow-bright the moor expands,
How shall your children clap their hands!
To make this earth our hermitage,
A cheerful and a changeful page,
God's bright and intricate device
Of days and seasons doth suffice.

ROBERT LOUIS STEVENSON

In the Mushroom Meadows.

Sun on the dewy grasslands where late the frost hath shone,
And lo, what elfin cities are these we come upon!
What pigmy domes and thatches, what Arab caravan,
What downy-roofed pagodas that have known no touch of man!
Are these the old-time meadows? Yes, the wildgrape scents the air;
The breath of ripened orchards still is incense everywhere;
Yet do these dawn-encampments bring the lurking memories
Of Egypt and of Burma and the shores of China Seas.

THOMAS WALSH

THE GARDEN OF CHILDHOOD

Daisy

BELLIS PERENNIS

Nature does not plant her flowers in carefully designed beds and borders. She spreads whole meadows with daisies and buttercups. She tosses a thousand Johnny-jump-ups on one bank and weaves the intricate tapestry of Mayapple leaves on another. Her forget-me-nots are reflected in brooklets rarely visited; her wild roses blow along sandy dunes by the sea. On deserts she plumps up cushions of saxifrages; in forests she sets the lady's-slipper and Jack-in-the-pulpit, the bloodroot, the Virgina bluebell.

She does not use our methods to weed or mulch or prune these wild gardens. Her rain and her sunshine, fog or drought sweep them impartially. Disease and pests are not combated; bird and bee are welcome.

And so is the child.

He may pick whatever he pleases wherever he pleases. He can trample a million violets or bluets, seeking a single arbutus, and discard a hundred heads of butter-and-eggs until he finds the one particular specimen which, under proper pressure, will open and shut its pouting cream and yellow lips in the dainty yawn.

If children love to range along the roadside or poke behind fences and hedges, emerging with a fistful of quickly wilting leaves and blossoms, it is not primarily because they are attracted by the esthetic or botanical features of their gatherings. It is because certain flowers are natural playthings, lending themselves to amusing manipulation. A child of three can string daisy heads to make a chain, or braid them, by their long stems, into a crown.

One of four can pluck the rays and read the future: "One I love, two I love, three I love, I say . . ." and then squeeze the yellow center into the palm of the hand, toss it into the air, catch the grains on the back of the hand and count the number of children which will follow those promises of love.

"Do you like butter?" What better way of finding the answer to this question than by holding a buttercup under the chin of a playmate and carefully determining if a golden glow is reflected?

How much more exciting than a paper chase to grope along the trail of red checkerberries, on and on, under the fallen pine needles.

The very name touch-me-not was irresistible. You simply had to touch the pod and watch it snap open as if released by a spring and send its seeds flying through the air.

Trumpet-flower ladies were easily contrived by making small slits in two of the petals and pulling out the curved stamens for arms. To make gentlemen, you cut the ruffle off the bottom, so they could dance—preferably on the top of a flat stump. The seed pods of the paulownia became long brown canoes which floated out of sight down a rivulet. It was good luck to call doodlebugs out of their holes, and in order to do this you knelt or lay so that your mouth was as close as possible to their hiding place. "Doodlebug,

doodlebug, your house is on fire," you sang over and over. The doodlebug—what *is* a doodlebug?—paid no attention to this warning. In fact, no doodlebug was ever seen as far as I know, but that did not prevent you being sure that some day he—or she—would certainly appear.

When a ladybird—a red bug with black spots—lighted on or near you, a similar incantation was uttered:

"Ladybird, ladybird, fly away home,
Your house is on fire and your children will burn."

Since it was accompanied by a wave of the hand, the ladybird was off like a shot.

If you tore the outer petals from a columbine flower, you could see the doves, feeding from the same dish. If you pulled a pansy apart, you could find the little old man sitting in the center. He is always cold, so he has to wrap himself in a yellow blanket, and his feet are in a long narrow foot-tub.

Violets have a hook where the stem and blossom meet, and when two of these are linked together, the game is to pull them apart like a wishbone and make a wish, which will come true for the one who pulls successfully.

Where the bee sucks, there sucks the child, and what syrup is sweeter than that which can be extracted from one of the flowers of a clover head? And speaking of clover, anyone knows its chief purpose is to produce an occasional four-leaved lucky one, which is worth hours of hunting, just as the chief merit of a wide blade of grass is that when held tightly between the thumbs of both hands and blown upon, it will emit a horrid screech. These are matters of tangible importance which graminologists are prone to overlook.

No child has to be shown how to pull apart the rubbery pod of the milkweed and set the silken fluff with its dark flat seeds floating down the wind. No child has to be taught how to suck the thin strong leaf of a maple into a kind of bubble gum in reverse and smack it smartly on the back of the hand so that it bursts with a pop.

However, it takes some practice before small fingers learn how to manipulate the thick succulent leaves of live-forever, separating the membrane on the under side until it is detached from the upper side, except along the serrated edges. Now, with the pressure of a fingernail, a semicircular opening is cut across the top, and into this you can blow until the leaf swells into a tiny sac. It is easy to see why it is sometimes called witch's money bag, but Aaron's-rod and midsummer men do very well also, and are certainly preferable to the dull name of sedum which grownups call it.

The August sun draws out the scent of drying hay and the whir of crickets as a little girl directs her steps to the brier patch behind the back fence. The burrs are just right to pull—big and green with sharp prickles. She picks the first gingerly, adds a second to it by the simple process of pressing them together. She makes a row, a double row, a triple, builds up the edges and trims them with those burrs which show downy purplish tufts. When it is further finished with a handle, she possesses a basket.

The little girl carries it carefully to her own room and puts it on the window sill, where it either stays until the burrs have dried to brown or is knocked off and swept away and in either case is forgotten. Nowadays the burrs do not seem as large as they did then. But perhaps that is because the fingers of the child were so small, so flexible, that they bear no relation to the hands of maturity.

And then all those ghostly growths of forest shade—cool, pallid Indian-pipes which, when picked by good children, retain their whiteness for hours, but when touched by naughty fingers immediately turn from brown to black—all of this entirely due to the morals of the gatherers and unassociated with such biological factors as body heat and manual pressure.

The mushrooms are of more varied shapes and sizes and colors. There are big red ones growing in the same damp shade as the Indian-pipes. Thin, fleshy, red-tinged gills are fascinating to touch, and you can pull the thick yellowish stems from the damp ground as easily as pulling a drumstick from a well-cooked chicken. There are hosts of toadstools which, crowded together, push aside a clod of grass and glitter briefly before they melt away. If you should put the tiniest morsel of the huge red mushrooms or the soft black-gilled toadstools into your mouth, you would fall over dead instantly, or perhaps not instantly but ultimately, after convulsions, paroxysms and fits.

But in open pastures, where the grass has been cropped close by grazing animals, there may be found those fairy rings of the mushrooms which are good to eat. The heads of the youngest ones are no bigger than the end of your thumb as they push up through the grassy earth. Under their caps the gills are white. The middle-age-sized ones have pink gills and in the old fellows the gills turn from brown to black. They are all great fun to pull, and your mother will be delighted when you come home bringing a hatful of them.

Puffballs, too, win approval in the kitchen, and when sliced and fried are perhaps even better than the mushrooms. Of course, they must be picked at the precise moment when they are large enough to be worth while, but not so large that they are leathery. However, they grow so rapidly that a few hours will bring them to perfection. If you forget to go back for a day or two, the one you marked may have swelled until it is bigger than a bald man's head, and when kicked will explode in a cloud of dark dust. This really is more fun than picking the big white ball which, even in a hot summer pasture, is eerily cool to the touch.

The instinct for personal adornment finds expression early. There are pine-needle necklaces, for instance. The needles grow from the twigs, two, three or five of them wrapped around the base by a thin paperlike sheath. Pull out all the needles but one and bend this over and tuck its tip into the sheath, and you have the first oval link of your chain. Or you can have earrings by pinching the winged seeds of the maple on the lobes of your ears. Anyone can have curls by slitting long dandelion stems.

These are some of the satisfactions children can gratify in nature's garden, whether that garden is a strip by the roadside, in a patch of woods, on a sunny upland or in a gritty tuft of vegetation by a railroad in a city. The pods and seeds, the leaves and blossoms that have afforded such moments of absorption are in a special world—a world for children, which persists through countless generations of them.

The leggy little girl who put a morning-glory atop a hollyhock and made a fine princess, or turned down the petals of a bleeding-heart to peer at the dainty pink lady in the dainty pink bathtub; the little boy who discovered under the protecting hood of the cuckoopint the standing lord or lady—are lost in the bodies of the plump practical matron and of the graying man regimented to his fixed hours of employment. While perhaps there is more of the little boy in the man than there is of the little girl in the woman, neither of them is the light-foot lad or the rose-leaf maiden. But the Jack-in-the-pulpit wordlessly exhorting the listening woods is just the same as he was decades ago. The doodlebug is just as coy.

The field may become a building site, the road may unroll its heavy weight of gravel and concrete through the forests, but the flowers thus displaced will leap beyond the boundaries and dance in other meadows and woodlands.

Keen are the tactile pleasures of avoiding the sharp bristles of the thistle while digging out the downy center, the prick of burrs, the stickiness of the casing around the base of the pine needles. Grownups wash their hands after handling flowers, but the stains and smells and the slippery juices are deliciously enjoyable to the child.

This pleasure reaches its intensest moments when you go out for water lilies, paddling a boat or perhaps poling a raft on a pond or along the edges of a lake.

The glisteningly white lily floats on the surface of the water and its flat green leaves float around it. The long rubberlike stem is attached to the thick muck at the bottom of the pond and when you pull it stretches before it snaps. You don't bother about the yellow pond lilies—they are more cuplike and coarser—it is only the white ones you want and you pull them up one by one, far more than you intend. The long stems dangle as you carry the armful into the house, dripping all over. It never occurs to you to float a single specimen in a shallow container. You merely jam the whole caboodle into a handy pitcher, shove it on the table, and run off to new adventures while the smooth and spicy fragrance fills the room.

Perhaps years later you will see in some tropical land the monstrous *Victoria regia,* whose flower may be a foot across and which blooms at night, exuding a scent like pineapple. The flower is lovely, but the leaves are incredible. They are absolutely circular, with turned up edges, and are so strong that they can carry a hundred and fifty pounds and not be submerged.

You will gaze at this with wonder, but feel no impulse to paddle out and tug at the curiously elastic stem. For to you a water lily is the one that floated on the ponds of childhood and which you yanked up and carted home and stuck in a pitcher and never remembered that it would close tight at sundown. This fabulous blossom a foot across is far too big for such a thing, and what would you do with a leaf bigger than a tray?

You may find pleasure in your garden as long as you live. Perhaps this is one of the few pleasures which does not diminish but intensifies as we grow older. But the fun of playing with flowers, the delight of feeling them, touching them, the half-frightened thrill of nibbling them—these are delights which pass with childhood.

Soon will the high midsummer pomps come on,
Soon will the musk carnations break and swell,
Soon shall we have gold-dusted snapdragon,
Sweet-William with his homely cottage smell,
And stocks in fragrant blow;
Roses that down the alleys shine afar,
And open jasmine-muffled lattices,
And groups under the dreaming garden-trees,
And the full moon and the white evening star . . .

MATTHEW ARNOLD

BY ANY OTHER NAME

Carnation

DIANTHUS CARYOPHYLLUS

There is a story about a harmless lunatic in a sanatorium whose chief—whose only—pleasure was to read plays. He would read current successes; he would read Shakespeare. Any dramatic text which was put into his hands kept him contented as long as its perusal lasted. The indulgent attendants gave him whatever books were on the shelves of the institution, and even borrowed from the local library. But, finally, there came a day when he had read everything immediately available and he became restless and irritable, continually demanding some volume of plays. At his wits' end, an attendant seized a New York telephone directory and thrust it into his hands, and was relieved to see him settle down quietly and begin to go through it, slowly, carefully, column after column, page after page. It kept him occupied for weeks and one day the attendant asked him with a smile how he liked the play.

"Oh, I know I shall enjoy it," replied the lunatic courteously, "but I must say it has a tremendously long list of characters."

Is there an amateur gardener who has not felt, on opening any book on botany, any manual, dictionary, encyclopedia or even seed catalogue, that the list of characters is tremendously long? Doubly so, since both the botanical name and the vernacular are given. Bewilderingly so, when these may contradict each other, as with the dogtooth violet, which is not a violet at all, but belongs to the lily family. The rose of Sharon (*Althea*) is not a rose but an hibiscus. Rose campion is a mullein pink (*Lychnis*); rose-of-heaven is also a pink (*Lychnis-coeli*). Confusion confounded, since the botanical name of one plant may be the popular name of another. The watercress is *Roripa nasturtium-aquaticum* and the common garden nasturtium is properly *Tropaeolum*. Still more confusion when the same nickname is given to entirely different flowers. In one locality the buttercup (*Ranunculus*) is called ragged robin, and in another locality the ragged robin is the cuckoo-flower (*Lychnis flos-cuculi*). Snow-on-the-mountain (*Euphorbia marginata*) is snow-in-summer and also milk-and-water.

No flower is too bourgeois to escape the burden of a nomenclature rivaling that of sons and daughters of European royalty. It would require a caligrapher like those who inscribed a Bible on a dime to crowd all of its names on the petals of a pansy. In England alone there are sixty, including heartsease, lady's-delight, love-in-idleness, Johnny-jump-up, kiss-me-at-the-garden-gate, herb-trinity, cuddle-me-to-you, tickle-my-fancy, kiss-me-ere-I-rise, kit-run-in-the-street. In Europe there are two hundred.

Botanists have worked out scientific classifications according to class, order, family, genus, species and variety, under names usually descriptive and usually derived from Greek or Latin. Such classification and terminology are universal, so that there need be no difficulty in recognizing and exchanging information about practically any plant anywhere in the world. Even if the words

hemselves may be cumbersome, their definition is clear. The generic name is like the family name or surname of a person—such
as Smith or Jones. The specific name, often an adjective, corre-
ponds to the baptismal name. Thus, *Viola tricolor* is the botanical
name for pansy, showing that it belongs to the genus *Viola,* the
pecies *tricolor.*

Too well we know that without this orderly arrangement we
may be lost when we try to buy seeds or plants or to look up information about the cultivation or diseases of a familiar plant. It is
like wandering around the city of New York, trying to locate kit-
run-in-the-street, instead of looking in the directory and finding
first *Viola* and then *tricolor.* The lunatic who studied the telephone
book may have had the right idea, after all.

In spite of this scholarly aid, there is a sentimental stubborn-
ness which keeps some old-fashioned names in our hearts and daily
speech. Foxglove, bleeding-heart, monkshood, snapdragon, shepherd's-purse, dusty miller, baby's-breath, red-hot poker, Dutchman's-pipe, smoke-bush are cozily descriptive. Sometimes the description applies in reverse. Old man (*Artemisia abrotanum*)
smells sweeter than is usual with most old men. Boy-love is certainly a euphemism for wormwood, although it is all too clear why
the same flower is also called maiden's ruin.

Sometimes names are associated with some former utilitarian
purpose: a branch of broom (*Cytisus scoparius*) was a handy thing
for sweeping the hearth. Some of the analogies have been lost
through the centuries. Thus, the bachelor's button—called blue
bonnet, cornflower, bluebottle, break-your-spectacles—is still occasionally in homely speech called logger. Probably few who use
the term know that a logger was an ancient battle weapon con-
sisting of an iron disk with a long handle. Conflict between two
such implements was coming to loggerheads—a common enough
phrase today.

Animals contribute their names. Duckweed, chickweed, cat-

nip, hawkweed, for obvious reasons, although one wonders wh.
kind of horse could manage to manipulate the prickly husk of th
horse-chestnut.

With others, the name came from their resemblance to som
part of a familiar fowl—cockscomb, hen-and-chickens, catkin
pussy willows, oxeye daisies, larkspur. There is an enormous grou
of plants called *Labiatae,* from the Latin word meaning lip, a
though, with the insouciance which characterizes such matters, th
cowslip belongs to quite a different family (*primulaceae*), whil
dragon's-mouth and lamb's-toe are both claimed by the orchi
family. The tulip does not refer to two lips, but was named fo
its resemblance to a colorful turban. "Tulipan" was medieva
Europe's spelling of the Arab word.

Some flowers were named for the time of their blooming—
Christmas rose, Lenten lily, Michaelmas daisy and calendula—thi
last a Roman nomenclature given it in a country where it bloomed
every month in the year. It is easy to trace daisy to day's eye
which is the form often found in Elizabethan literature.

There are hundreds of legends, myths and folk tales as t
how flowers got their names, but these fables are rarely as pretty
as the names themselves. Meadowsweet, traveler's-joy, forget-me-
not, virgin's-bower, sweet sultan do very well without any ex-
planatory note.

The Bible has been recalled in many epithets. Aaron's-rod,
Jacob's ladder, Solomon's-seal, Star-of-Bethlehem are still with us,
although Grace-of-God (*Hypericum*), Gethsemane (*Orchis*) and
hallelujah (*Oxalis*) have been forgotten.

It is curious that some of the most appropriate and pronounceable designations have been lost. Thus, the old-fashioned
English name for asparagus was sperage and had a logical derivation, for formerly in the Roman Catholic churches in Southern
Europe the feathery sprays of this plant were dipped in holy water
and used for asperging the congregation. It is puzzling that this

word, taken directly from the Latin *aspergo*—which means a sprinkling—should have been replaced by the longer and less graphic Greek—*asparagos*.

Neither is such replacement a matter of euphony. Colloquial nicknames are by no means always the prettiest. Cancer-root (*Epiphegus*), lousewort (*Pedicularis*), bladderwort (*Utricularia*), bugloss (*Anchusa*), nipplewort (*Lapsana*), toadflax (*Linaria*), woadwaxen (*Genista*), fetid marigold (*Dysodia*), shinleaf (*Pyrola*) (equally unappetizing as consumption weed or canker lettuce), liverleaf (*Hepatica*), have little to recommend them. Tickseed does better as *Coreopsis,* sneezewort as *Achillea* and mugwort as *Artemisia.* Kidneywort, which is also called coyote bush, chaparral broom, and squaw waterweed enter civilized society as *Baccharis,* and mule-fat creeps in under the same kindly name.

Incidentally, the suffix "wort," which is disagreeable to some ears, has a sturdy lineage from the Anglo-Saxon wyrt, which is simply a plant.

Sometimes both the botanical and the vernacular are equally pleasing. *Aquilegia* is as musical as columbine, and *Nigella* as dainty as love-in-a-mist or little-maiden-in-the-green. *Lunaria* is named for the moon, which it suggests in shape and sheen, and this is quite as descriptive as its many fond nicknames: honesty, poor-man's-shilling, silver dollar, penny flower, moonwort, satinpod, satin-flower.

Some of the botanical names are mercifully brief enough to have become popular. Thus iris, kalmia, daphne, clematis and verbena are interchangeable in scientific as well as colloquial use. Zinnia, cosmos, phlox, anemone are the same everywhere, while others have been so slightly altered as to be instantly recognizable, such as hyacinthus, saxifraga, tulipa, rosa, lupina, lilium.

Still others have been literally translated. *Helianthus* is sunflower. *Chrysogonum* is golden-knee. The dandelion holds a modest distinction in that it means the same in every language—the tooth of the lion—although it is not certain if this is from the shape of the leaf, the whiteness of the root, or because the lion was the symbol of the sun, of which this is the tiny replica. The mayflower is another individualist. Found only in North America—and, oddly, in Japan—it belongs to the heath family (*Ericaceae*). Since these syllables stick in the throat, it is commonly called the arbutus. The pilgrims called it the mayflower and mayflower it remains, although it has no connection with the English May, which is the hawthorn. The only mayflower mentioned in English gardening books is lady's-smock, or meadowcress. To be sure, the *Claytonia* of eastern North America is sometimes called mayflower, but as it is also called grass-flower, good-morning-spring and spring beauty, and since it belongs to the family *Portulacaceae*, the matter is decidedly confused.

Conscientious botanists, in their endeavor to acknowledge the services of a discoverer of some plant or to localize it, too often add what seems like further intricacy.

We are willing—we are glad—to recall the great Linnaeus in the modest bell-like *Linnea*, faintly streaked with pink, which he so loved that he had it painted on his own coffee cup and saucer.

It is more difficult for the layman to feel similar sentiment for personalities preserved only in specialized archives, such as the information that *Magnolia* was named for the early French botanist Pierre Magnol, and *Magnolia fraseri* for the botanist Fraser, who was one of the first to find this species. Dr. Sarrazin of Quebec, who sent the first American pitcher plant to Europe, is honored in the order *Sarraceniaceae*. *Kerria* was named for W. Kerr, a plant collector; *Kalmia* for Peter Kalm, the Swedish botanist. We are inclined to snub Alexander Macleay, Colonial Secretary to Australia, for we usually call the *Macleaya* the *Bocconia* or plume poppy or tree celandine.

As for the *canadensis, virginica, caroliniana, americana,* etc., which indicate where a plant was first discovered, these no longer have any but historical significance, since most of them now grow in many other places.

We do, indeed, owe a debt to the German botanist, Franz Carl Mertens, since *Mertensia,* which recalls him, is far prettier than the original lungwort. Anders Dahl, the Swedish botanist, should be thanked for the short and pronounceable name of the dahlia.

Nowadays so many varieties of so many flowers are named for so many people of transitory distinction that they are honored by the flower instead of the flower being honored by them.

It seems there is no fixed rule. Sometimes the colloquial name is more descriptive and easier to pronounce, and sometimes the botanical. No one can claim *Scabiosa* is a flattering appellation for a most obliging flower, even if it is explained that it refers to its power to cure the itch and not to cause it. But mourning bride and pincushion-flower, which have the merit of quaint descriptiveness, seem to be yielding ground to the ugly pathological syllables. Rhododendron is awkward, but rolls glibly from every tongue.

Illogicality pervades the whole vocabulary. It is easy to assume that mignonette was originally French, but actually the French have always dignified this pet by its botanical *Reseda.*

Almost the only people who can unreservedly approve the present floral vocabulary are the crossword puzzle addicts and anagramists. To them *Xiphium, Yedoensis* and *Zingiberaceae* are godsends.

But some of us who are too busy gardening to play anagrams regret that certain of the most delightful names in our literature should have passed from daily usage. Why should the eglantine, which still survives in French, have been discarded in English? Why should the gillyflower (juillet-flower) which is such a pretty part of English prose and poetry, where it is synonymous with carnation, have been replaced in America by stock?

Canterbury bells, snowdrops and hollyhocks still hold their own, but one wonders what happened to bobbing Joan and blooming Sally who rollicked down the centuries? Who were Sweet Cicely and Creeping Jenny, and who, oh, who, was Joe-Pye-weed? Was he just Joe or Joe Pye? Why do we exclaim, when we see the tall plant with big tousled rufus head standing in rough thickets beside the road, "Halloa! There's Joe-Pye-weed," and not, "Oh, there is some *Eupatorium purpureum*," or even, "See the purple boneset!" No, it is Joe-Pye-weed who has pushed aside the ancient King of Pontus, Eupator Mithridates, who is supposed to have discovered a medicinal use for the plant named after him.

Who was that Robin who was so ragged? Was he the same poor fellow who had to be shaken out of sleep every morning, and thus became wake-robin? (Incidentally, wake-robin is *Trillium* in the United States and *Arum* in England.)

The rose holds its secure place both in our gardens and in our language. Even its connections are clearly traceable. Thus, *sub rosa* comes from the time when the Romans had a rose painted on the ceilings of their banqueting halls to remind the guests that whatever roistering or indiscreet speech took place was to be kept secret when they left the hall. Later it was a custom for a papal rose to be fixed over the confessional to emphasize the same obligation.

These fascinating speculations occur to us only occasionally, when our hands or minds are idle. Those who have worked in their gardens through many seasons call their flowers what they please. Those who are planning their first border may start properly and give each plant its proper botanical name and thereby find themselves able to use reference books intelligently and to chat with other flower lovers the world over. Too many of us will continue to jumble English, Latin, French with the intimate nicknames of our locality.

Probably poets will be faithful to asphodel in preference to narcissus.

I wholeheartedly subscribe to the practice of using botanical nomenclature. But, nevertheless, I sometimes find myself wondering what became of those girls—Nancy Pretty, Sweet Alice and Delicate Bess. I shall never cease to be intrigued by Joe-Pye-weed. (*Was* he Joe Pye or just plain Joe?) And I shall always wish I had seen with my own eyes the wholesome smiling face and trim form of the lad who was worthy to be called Sweet William.

The Strongest Poison ever known
Came from Caesar's Laurel Crown.

WILLIAM BLAKE

The Turks who passed their Days in Gardens here, will have Gardens also hereafter; and delighting in Flowers on Earth, must have Lilies and Roses in Heaven. In Garden Delights it is not easy to hold a Mediocrity; that insinuating Pleasure is seldom without some Extremity. The Ancients venially delighted in flourishing Gardens. Many were Florists that knew not the true use of a Flower. And in Pliny's Days none had directly treated of that Subject. Some commendably affected Plantations of venomous Vegetables; some confined their delights unto single Plants; and Cato seemed to dote upon Cabbage. While the ingenius Delight of Tulipists, stands saluted with hard language, even by their own Professors.

From "The Garden of Cyrus,"

SIR THOMAS BROWNE

POISON GARDEN

Leaf of Laurel

LAURUS NOBILIS

". . . While King Attalus lives for his poisonous plantations of aconites, henbane, hellebore and plants hardly admitted within the walls of Paradise . . ." interpolates Sir Thomas Browne, and goes on to the more splendid garden of Cyrus.

Now, we know more or less about Cyrus, both in fact and legend, but this King Attalus who indulged in a singular and unholy passion for poisonous plants—what kind of man was he? For what uses did he nurture his noxious establishment? This brief reference stirs up a miasma of evil. We imagine the murderous face of King Attalus gloating over his mephitic floral and arboreal concentration camp—tearing off blossoms, crushing leaves, grinding seeds, exhuming roots, distilling the essence of death.

A Poison Garden! What strange degeneration of delight! Did King Attalus, like Hamlet's uncle, creep up and drop poison into the ear of his sleeping kinsman whom he is supposed to have murdered and whom he did undoubtedly succeed? Did he try all sorts of hellish experiments on his slaves and watch their death writhings in glee? Did he, in lighter mood, meet his guests with a hypocritical smile and toss leis of poison ivy around their necks? Was the periphery of this plantation strewn with the bleached bones of lambs who had nibbled *Kalmia angustifolia,* and the corpses of little boys and girls who had popped the seeds of *Laburnum anagyroides* into their mouths?

The location of the Kingdom of Pergamus is almost as obscure as the peculiarities of its last King, dead for eighteen hundred years.

Pricked by curiosity to investigate further, we manage to ascertain that "négligeant ensuite sa personne, il laissa croître sa barbe et ses cheveux, ne se couvrique de vêtements sales et usés," which merely heightens the horrid picture. And what did the garden itself look like, sprouting shoots of venomous green and harboring only those plants which had within them the power for destruction?

From this so different century and in this so different climate we may permit our fancy to reconstruct those beds and borders without being unduly hampered by matters of temperature, soil and season.

In the spring it had poppies—oceans of them with their gray-green laciniated leaves and flowers of scarlet, white, pink, purple and yellow. Delphinium rose behind the poppies, in tall spires, and larkspur of lesser show. Monkshood lifted its panicles, blue and purple, white and yellow. Belladonna rang its flowery bells.

As the season progressed, the glisteningly white angel trumpets—the datura—unfurled in the morning sun and folded themselves away with exquisite precision in the late afternoon. In the shade there stood cuckoopint, which, as if that name were not pretty enough, is also called lords-and-ladies, Solomon's lily and, in England, wake-robin.

In the late spring there was foxglove—the finger flower—white, purple, yellow, spotted.

Still later in the calendar the autumn crocus—meadow saffron—pushed its sharp point above the earth and opened its mauve or lavender petals.

When the season for other flowers was over, in Pergamus a white rose, nearly stemless, appeared amid the evergreen leaves of the hellebore—perhaps even then called Christmas rose.

The flower garden, we must admit, was not unlike our own, except that with a kingly treasury to maintain it and a king neglecting the affairs of state to tend it, it was probably far handsomer than ours.

The flowers were only a part of this regal plantation. There were shrubs and trees. The oleander decked itself with immaculate rosettes. The rhododendrons shook out their great balls of white or rose. The glossy leaves of laurel glinted under the trees. *Cannabis* was conspicuously placed, and near it the vigorous poke plant spread its strong leaves. Again disregarding geography, we can add groups of cinchona and coca plants.

Some such assembly might have been the laboratory of King Attalus, specializing in poisons, and so absorbed in his botanical studies that he could not pause long enough to have his beard trimmed or his hair cut or change his dirty clothes.

If he had planted these flowers and shrubs and trees not because they were poisonous but because they were beautiful, he could hardly have chosen better.

Of course, they were no more poisonous as they budded and bloomed and faded than are their counterparts today. Few, indeed, are plants whose mere touch is harmful—such as certain ivies and sumac, and occasionally the cypripedium or pink lady's-slipper. Nettles sting, and in this day of well-classified allergies it is possible to assemble quite a list of plants which are irritating to susceptible lungs and nostrils. But most of the flowers in King

Attalus' garden had no baneful effects until he had diligently worked upon them. Since people do not usually chew the leaves or suck the juices or champ the stems or masticate the roots of their ornamental flowers and shrubs, they can live among them for a lifetime and never even know of their hidden virulence.

But King Attalus knew and spent a great deal of time and endless labor increasing this knowledge. No trouble was too great and he was sustained by his perverted ambitions to curse future generations.

As he carefully staked his tall monkshood, he liked to remember that it yielded the aconite such as was in the cup which Medea—who did not bother to conceal her penchant for murder—prepared for Theseus; that this was the draught which was given to those old men on the Aegean island of Ceos when they were too feeble to be of further working value. Did he look forward to the time when the red men of the Americas would fight the white men from Spain and England with arrows, darts and spears dipped in the deadly poison?

There are more than a hundred species of Aconitum, but without doubt the favorite of King Attalus was *Aconitum napelles,* for this was the chief source of the drug. This is our favorite, also, for it is the handsomest of them all. And if the classical name is too stilted and monkshood is too fanciful, we can call it wolfsbane, which manages to convey two unpleasant suggestions in two brief syllables. There is no visible feature to betray its potential malevolence. It is not dangerous to pick or handle. But when King Attalus extracted the juices he possessed a silent and handy means of dispatching his victims.

Then the belladonnas, with their bell-shaped purplish-red flowers and their black and fatal seeds—*Atropa belladonna*—fittingly named for that one of the three Fates who cut the thread of life, must have been the choice of King Attalus. Perhaps he would have approved its other name—deadly nightshade—for it grows from "the insane root that takes the reason prisoner," and in later centuries would be used by the Scots under Macbeth to destroy their enemy Danes.

As for the poppies, we can assume that the one which merited his attention was the *Papaver somniferum,* for the juice from the unripe pods yields opium. Was it to instil a lethal appetite and craving in whole continents of the human race, and reduce them to degradation that King Attalus bent his energies? To precipitate wars, reward smugglers and undermine morale?

The *Cannabis sativa,* or hemp plant, was one of his favorites, for the dried flower tops are made into hashish, which horribly enslaves its victims. Today these flower tops are used to make marijuana cigarettes. Thus the same plant may incite a man to murder and obligingly furnish the material for the rope to hang him. Certainly there must have been *Cannabis* in the garden of Attalus.

The ruinous potentialities of the coca plant must have won it room in the collection. The small white flowers are not particularly showy, but if you chew enough of the leaves and keep at it long enough, you can wreck your body and your mind, as is proved by those poor Indians in Peru who become addicts of the anesthetizing habit and finally end up—wasted and stupefied— public charges and private nuisances.

The hemlock was not our evergreen tree but a rankly growing herb with an insignificant white flower—*Conium maculatum* —the poison hemlock which killed Socrates.

With all these things, along with henbane and hellebore, which Sir Thomas Browne mentions and which set us off on this whole speculation, King Attalus had plenty of materials from which to make his concoctions. With such subtle weapons at his command, it is not surprising to read that he made himself odious by his cruelty to his relations, or that he finally developed hypochondria and a persecution complex and was suspicious of all his subjects and every member of his court.

These references are merely in passing. No historian seems to have given King Attalus and his unique garden any detailed attention. However, if we continue to hunt down volumes and turn pages, we can pick up a few more bits of information.

It seems that King Attalus III came by his interest logically, for the family of Attalus were exceptionally enthusiastic and efficient husbandmen. They admired Greek science and learning in general and scientific agriculture in particular. Attalus III compiled a textbook on the subject in which he attempted to adapt the theories of the Greek scientists to conditions as they existed in Asia Minor. When Varo and Columella and Pliny made out their lists of writers on agriculture, it is notable that most of them (during the Hellenistic period) were natives of Asia Minor or the larger Greek islands and places on the Thracian coasts, and all of them were connected in one way or another with the Kingdom of Pergamus. Our King Attalus III collected a library, wrote books and —ah, here we have it at last—"et inventa des rémèdes cités par Celse et Galien."

Could it be that King Attalus III was not primarily interested in poison as a death weapon, but in extracting from plants those drugs and medicines whose purpose is not to kill but to cure?

If this were so—assuming this were so—how different his garden appears now in our imagination. There grow the poppies, but the juice which Attalus so skilfully distils is that narcotic which wafts sufferers from pain to blessed release from it. Therefore, it is named for Morpheus, who was the son of sleep and the god of dreams.

The belladonna has gentler uses than medication, for its very name reminds us that the beautiful women of Italy used it to enlarge and beautify the pupils of their eyes. Still other uses transcend the corporeal altogether, for *Atropa mandraga* of the same genus has been sold for centuries for love philters. Perhaps this is what King Attalus—a sentimentalist at heart—was experimenting to find: not a drug to drive men insane but to satisfy the vanity of ladies and to soothe the pangs of love. Did he look still further into the future and genially decide to furnish detective story writers with that bottle of aconite without which they could hardly ply their trade, or their readers could hardly drowse off to sleep?

The kind-hearted king doubtless grieved that excessive chewing of the leaves of the coca shrub destroys the body and stupefies the mind. But before that grim finale it brings to many a poor Indian, trotting over the highlands of Peru, the only pleasure he is ever to know. It is the custom of these Indians to carry a little leather pouch filled with these leaves and to make them into a ball. They add a bit of slaked lime to improve the taste, and with such a ball tucked inside their cheeks they feel an access of strength and lose all sense of hunger. They can trot for barren miles under otherwise intolerable burdens, sustained, temporarily, by the drug which anesthetizes pain and quickens the mind. Against the hundreds of obscure Indians who have destroyed themselves through the habit, King Attalus set hundreds of thousands who have been grateful for cocaine when under the surgeon's knife or the dentist's drill.

King Attalus had a strong sense of reverence and therefore he honored the hemlock which answered the final and most baffling question of Socrates. The laurel he planted was not the *Laburnum anagyroides* to kill sheep, but the *Laurus nobilis* to wreathe the brows of heroes.

We can picture him carefully collecting the beautifully marked but lethal seeds of the castor oil plant, lest dear little children be tempted to taste them. Since they sometimes rebel at the wholesome but disagreeable taste of castor oil, he indulgently cultivated *Cascara sagrada* to serve the same necessity. He added licorice to soothe their coughs, and arnica for their sprains and bruises.

Obviously, the garden of Attalus has been misnamed, and

because of the misnomer he has been misjudged. In all probability it was merely an herb garden of greater dimension and variety than most, and yielding fascinating material to the experimenter

For all gardens were originally herb gardens, and were cultivated not primarily for their beauty or their fragrance but for medicinal purposes.

Not so long ago—not even half a century ago—a pharmacist manufactured, or had his apprentices manufacture, his own drugs, and a pharmacy bore slight resemblance to our drug store with its soft drink counter, its display of cosmetics, candies, pocket editions of detective stories and its radio and juke boxes.

Drugs and drugs only—in the form of elixirs and tinctures, powders and pills, plasters and ointments—were the only merchandise, and these were arranged upon the shelves in alphabetical order which was not unlike a garden catalogue. Ambergris, balm-of-Gilead, belladonna, cubeb, camomile, foxglove, gentian, hemlock, lavender, mandrake, monkshood, musk and myrrh, rosemary and rue, sweet marjoram and thyme.

Their curative claims were prodigious. Thus, a few ripening seeds of henbane could deprive a man of his senses but smoked in a pipe relieved toothache. Bittersweet or woody nightshade cured asthma, camomile soothed the stomach pains. *Euphorbia*—purple spurge—removed warts, and ground ivy—*Nepeta glecoma*—when dropped in wine removed white spots from the eyes. The root of the yellow flag incited sneezing in case of headache, and the autumn crocus relieved rheumatism and gout.

A curious doctrine of signatures developed. This depended on discovering the medicinal use of a plant from something in its external appearance which resembled the disease it would cure.

Thus aspen, since its leaves shake, must be good for shaking palsy. Saxifrage grew in cracks in rocks and, therefore, would crack the deposits known as stone in the bladder. Knots of scrophularia were prescribed for scrofulous swellings, bloodroot for dysentery, turmeric for jaundice since it was the color of jaundiced skin. Wood sorrel, since it has a heart-shaped leaf, was a heart restorative, liverwort corrected inactive liver, bryony cured dropsy because its root suggested a swollen foot.

The plasters, ointments and tinctures and powders did not confine their beneficial effects to the body, but ministered also to the inner man. Pimpernel revived the spirits, antirrhinum destroyed charms and rendered maledictions harmless, and ashes made from the root of the mandrake restored gray hair to its original color, and may thus be considered a strengthener of morale.

This was a short step to diabolism and magic. Deadly nightshade caused the eater to see ghosts; henbane threw its victims into convulsions; bittersweet caused skin eruptions; meadow saffron and black hellebore racked the nerves and caused the victim to swell. Bryony set the nose bleeding; eyebright sowed rheumatism in the bones.

Some of these beliefs are ancient indeed. In 300 B.C. Theophrastus wrote a history of plants and described more than five hundred used in the treatment of disease. The elder Pliny described a thousand.

Most extraordinary of all was Shên Nung, the Chinese celestial agriculturist. In 2737 B.C.—the exactness of the date proves its authenticity—he compiled a materia medica. In one single day he discovered seventy poisonous plants and their antidotes. Nung had an unfair advantage over Attalus and, indeed, over all experimenters who were to come after him, for he had a stomach with transparent walls through which he would watch and study his digestive processes.

There are other famous names associated with poisons. Mithridates VI, Eucaptor, King of Pontus, who lived about the same time as King Attalus, is said to have so saturated his body with poisons that he believed none could injure him, which was highly convenient for a potentate surrounded by enemies plotting against his life. It may have been this legend which gave Hawthorne the plot for "Rappaccini's Daughter" and, more recently, Richard Garnet his story "The Poison Maid."

To come back to King Attalus who started us on all this. Instead of being a sadist, he now emerges as a scientist.

So wholeheartedly did he devote himself to his laudable experiments that he had no time to play the dandy.

A sentence buried in a paragraph dealing with other personages happens to mention that besides being a botanist, a chemist and a writer of agricultural books, he showed further versatility by experimenting with the melting of metals, and by modeling in wax, copper and bronze.

To crown it all, he was so filial that when he decided to erect a tomb to his mother, he himself put his hand to the project. As usual, he applied all his energies to the labor and while at it suffered a sunstroke from which he died, after having reigned five years. He left the Kingdom of Pergamus to the people of Rome.

Good King Attalus!

Which, like unruly children, make their sire
Go, bind thou up yon dangling apricocks,
Stoop with oppression of their prodigal weight;
Give some supportance to the bending twigs.
Go thou, and like an executioner,
Cut off the heads of too fast growing sprays,
That look too lofty in our commonwealth;
All must be even in our government.

SHAKESPEARE

BEGINNER'S GARDEN

Hollyhock
ALTHAEA ROSEA

There are rock gardens and wild-flower gardens; green gardens and desert gardens; white gardens and blue gardens; herb gardens and bird gardens; and there is one that is different from any of these.

This is your garden.

I am always touched when I see a beginning gardener setting forth with a great array of new tools, or an inadequate assortment of old ones, to dig up or scratch up a large plot or a small one, and to scatter seeds for annuals or dig holes for perennials, shrubs and trees.

It is a glorious venture, like first love, like marriage, like a trip to an unknown country, like the initial appearance in print or on the stage.

The veteran gardener is the first to cheer the recruit. Advice, clippings, seedlings, bulbs, plants are showered upon him. This is not because there is any assurance that these tentative plantings will blossom forth in complete triumph, but because those who have experienced the joy of gardening know that there is no other joy which precisely parallels it. They see the novice go down on his knees—a position which is to become increasingly customary —with the satisfaction of a proselytizer who witnesses one more convert to the cause.

Of course, the novice does not know what he is in for, but the reason he is to be congratulated is because he is embarking upon a quest whose reward is certain, since this reward is in the doing rather than in the result.

There are many different kinds of excitements and pleasures in store for the beginning gardener. There is the good, hearty, sweating tiredness that comes from physical labor. There is the elation of seeing the first crocus prick through the earth or the first rose unfurl. There may even be the astonishment of actually producing a nicely balanced plot filled with masses and masses of flowers—tall ones in back, low ones in front—all harmonizing— more or less—and following in proper order.

Although this consummation is by no means certain, the beginning gardener dashes ahead with vision of a display which will rival a professional flower show. And when he looks at his resulting assortment of too much foliage and too little bloom, at magentas that should have been pink, at giants that should have been dwarfs, of stragglers that should have been bushy, he loves them all. He loves them because he has known and handled them from the time they were minutissimic seeds, each containing not only its plant but concentrated food sufficient for its needs until it could send out roots; from the time they were amorphous lumps of root, protesting at being exposed to light; or non-committal bulbs stubbornly wrapped in their tight scalelike leaves. Each one promised perfection and it must be admitted that some have defaulted. But the sanguine gardener is sure he can improve upon this ratio next year.

It is cheering that such homely sentiment can persist in our present mechanized world. It is cheering that while there are superb musical records of the greatest operas and symphonies available to almost everyone, there are still thousands of music teachers who find plenty of pupils who gladly and faithfully practice interminably in order to hammer and bang and squeal and screech on their own instruments. They do not claim that the sounds they produce are comparable with those of concert performers, but they have a grand time making them. And so it is, and so it should be, with the home gardener, making mistakes, fumbling and bumbling among his flowers and finding in his care of them a special delight.

If he does not find this delight, I see no reason for his continuing to garden. His labor, if joyless, defeats its purpose as far as he is concerned, and economically and esthetically it can be dispensed with by the community. It is not even necessary as a social passport, for there are garden clubs which elect members who have not as much as a window box, but who are good organizers or just congenial friends. There is no obligation to have a garden, and the remarkable thing is that so many people have one or, rather, that they continue to have one, despite the deterring danger signals continually flapped in their faces.

The beginning gardener might well be aghast at those articles and books which go after the matter as if it were a grim and grinding business, to be pushed through out of some sense of duty, and which discuss the relative values of fertilizers as if they were assembling a stock pile for an atomic bomb. He might well feel depressed by those recitals—supposedly humorous—of the pests, blights and droughts, and back-breaking, fingernail-breaking toil which await him. But if the instinct to garden is in his soul, he does not, having put his hand to the spade, turn back. As well expect a radiant bride to shy away from the altar because of spiteful croakings that marriage is only a ceaseless scuffle with cleaning and cooking, and motherhood only a succession of anxieties, disciplines and expenses.

The gardener is too busy looking forward to new successes to brood over past failures.

This looking forward—which is one of the mainsprings of a happy life—is generously accorded the beginning gardener. Neither does it diminish as he grows older.

I once journeyed several hundred miles to the funeral of a friend and, arriving there a few hours before the services, went into her garden. For a long time she had known that she would not recover from her mortal malady, but the last morning she had been able to be outdoors she had trimmed and shaped a recently planted small-leaved euonymus. It was spreading its little branches espaliered against the wall, neat and glossy and prepared to grow symmetrically as she had intended. My friend knew she would never see the lovely tracery covering the wall, but she acknowledged the persistence of life, and as I stood before the work of her hands I acknowledged it, too.

This belief in the future gives quietness to the mind and buoyancy to the body, so that we are often astonished at the vigor with which the very aged apply themselves to some garden task, not thinking of it as a task but as a pleasure. For while they are thus occupied, they are not conscious of being either old or young but only of being part of surging, growing life.

For perhaps the pleasure which sinks most deeply into our inmost selves with the succeeding years is the sense of communication with a living world which supplements but does not infringe upon our human one. Flowers bud, open, wither, fall. Plants flourish or sicken, recover or are cut down. They draw in their nourishment from earth, air, water and sun. They attract birds and bees, are pollinated, make seed, scatter it, in a cycle as irresistible and as precisely synchronized as the movements of the stars and planets. They are part of the rhythm of life, just as we are part of it, and they companion us through every mood. This is the special blessing which belongs to those who work in their own gardens.

There are people who have no taste for gardening, and I can see no reason for apology in this admission. Any nurseryman can set out shrubs to redeem a bare foundation. Any florist—almost any grocery store—sells flowers as handsome as those we can raise and considerably cheaper, taking everything into account. Your grounds outside may be as satisfactory and your vases and bowls inside may be as effective if you never put your hand to a trowel. And if you yourself lose that companionship which comes only from daily association with a garden, you are not even aware of your loss.

Some of the Eastern religions make no attempt to proselytize, believing that when a human soul is ready to embrace certain tenets, it will seek them and find them. The true gardener unconsciously shares this attitude. He feels no impulse to debate the rewards of his chosen course. He offers no rebuttal to those outside the charmed association who refer to gardening only in terms of tedious labor, as if there were any art, profession or business which does not require preliminary—and usually accompanying—drudgery. Weeding and watering demand no greater physical exertion than golf or tennis; than swimming, skiing or any outdoor sport. Poring over seed catalogues is no more time-consuming than playing bridge, and going to flower shows no less worthy—and no more so—than going to horse shows and ball games.

It is merely a matter of preference, and the devotees of this or any recreation do not need encouragement and are blithely immune to discouragement.

No matter how many years one has gardened, there is always more—a great deal more—to be learned, and this exhilaration which is tasted by the recruit is fully savored by the old campaigner.

When Thomas Jefferson was forty-three, he wrote to his daughter, "There is not a sprig of grass that shoots uninteresting to me." And a quarter of a century later he wrote again, "I am still devoted to the garden. But although an old man I am but a young gardener."

For all true gardeners are only beginners, and confidence in the future lightens their way like Pentecostal tongues of fire.

Thus it is that the gardener needs no urgings and heeds no warnings, but from the first awkward essay with the spade to the last expert pruning of an evergreen, he is conscious, with gratitude deeper than ever did plummet sound, that he is blessed.

Our blessed Saviour chose the Garden for his Oratory, and dying, for the place of his sepulchre; and we do avouch for many weighty causes, that there are none more fit to bury our dead in than in our Gardens and Groves, where our Beds may be decked with verdant and fragrant flowers, Trees and Perennial Plants, the most natural and instructive Hieroglyphics of our expected Resurrection and Immortality.

JOHN EVELYN

A garden inclosed is my sister, my spouse; a spring shut up, a fountain sealed. Thy plants are an orchard of pomegranates, with pleasant fruits; camphire, with spikenard; spikenard and saffron; calamus and cinnamon, with all trees of frankincense; myrrh and aloes, with all the chief spices; a fountain of gardens, a well of living waters, and streams from Lebanon. Awake, O north wind; and come, thou south; blow upon my garden, that the spices thereof may flow out. Let my beloved come into his garden, and eat his pleasant fruits.

THE SONG OF SOLOMON

SAINTS, SINNERS AND THE SCRIPTURES

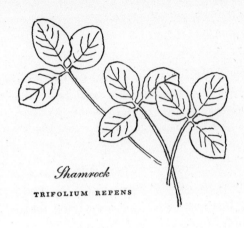

Shamrock

TRIFOLIUM REPENS

"From the fig leaf in Genesis to the star wormwood in the Apocalypse are variously interspersed expressions from plants advantaging the significancy of the text," writes Sir Thomas Browne, and he continues the subject of plants in Scripture at length and in the majestic style formed by study of these same Scriptures.

About the same time that Sir Thomas was writing his *Garden of Cyrus,* the botanist Olaf Celsius was taking a trip from his native Sweden through the Holy Land for the purpose of studying the flora, and he put his carefully annotated findings in a big book named *Hierbotanicon.*

Only a few people read Sir Thomas Browne today. Perhaps only a few read the Scriptures diligently. And even fewer tackle Celsius. But in the two centuries since the *Hierbotanicon* appeared other students of botany and the Bible have been hard at the same task. Philologists are still absorbedly re-examining the oldest Hebrew and Greek texts in their different translations and versions. Botanists are still traveling over Egypt, the Arabian Desert and

Palestine to verify and classify the plants indigenous to thes[e] regions. Conscientious preachers are still endeavoring to give th[e] correct theological interpretation of Biblical verse and vegetation[.]

These are matters for specialists, and most of us are conten[t] to leave them in their hands.

But the least scholarly among us yield to occasional curiosi[-]ties, particularly about those miraculous plants which, as children[,] we pictured usually incorrectly but with literal vividness. We al[l] have some mental pictures of the lilies of the field, the crown o[f] thorns, the mock scepter of reed at the trial before Pontius Pilate— pictures based, quite naturally, on the assumption that these wer[e] the same lilies and thorns and reeds found in our own fields.

Therefore, we may be astonished if we chance to read that the lilies so often mentioned were not white—for the white lily is[s] not native to Palestine—but red, like our Turk's-cap lily (*Lilium chalcedonicum*), and it was this scarlet flower which Solomon com- pared to the lips of his beloved. And now, in 1948, H. L. and A. L. Moldenke come along with their *Plants of the Bible* for further readjustment. The poppy anemone (*Anemone coronaria*), which blooms in great profusion in scarlet, purple, blue and gold, is probably the Bible lily about which Jesus said, "Solomon in all his glory was not arrayed like one of these."

As for those other flowers of the field so often mentioned, there were in Palestine in Bible times, as there are today, narcissi, crocus, tulips, amaryllis and iris, although the rose was probably the oleander, the rose tree of the Greeks (*Rhododendron*), which grows in all the warmer parts of the country by pools and streams and is especially plentiful in Jericho.

It may be that the next time we arrange the Christmas crèche or glance at a nativity in a church or in a shop window at that festival time, our eyes will rest a moment on the straw in the manger. On that first Christmas in Bethlehem, the manger in

which the Virgin laid her little Son was doubtless softened by the
herblike grass which is common to the region. Because of this, the
French call it sainfoin or holy hay, which is rather prettier than
our alfalfa or lucerne or the botanical *Onobrychis viciaefolia*. Of
the innumerable legends which have gathered around that manger
is the one that when the wise men came to worship, Mary lifted
the Child so that they might see Him better, and where His head
had lain on the sainfoin there was a circle of blossoms. For this
reason, devout Italians line their Christmas mangers with such
grasses as are green at that season or use moss as a substitute for
the holy hay.

Whatever kind of palm leaf we receive on Palm Sunday, we
will remember the one that still rises in the orchards and olive
groves of Philistia and Sidon, and is often seen in Arabia and
Egypt. In ancient times it grew throughout the whole valley of
the Jordan, from the shores of Gennesaret to the Dead Sea. It grew
in Bethany and on the Mount of Olives, so that it was natural it
should be referred to often in both the Old and New Testaments.

In early days in England, when it was not possible to get
genuine palm leaves, it was the custom to use willow branches or
yew branches for the service on the Sunday before Easter, and to
call these palms, which has brought confusion enough to many an
English child.

If the lilies of the Bible may have been anemones, and the
roses, oleanders, and the palms, in England, branches of willow or
yew, what about hyssop, which cleaned the body of the leper and
the soul of the repentant, and wetted the sponge raised to the lips
of Jesus on the Cross? Hyssop grows in our own herb gardens
(*Hyssopus officinalis*), but we are informed with positiveness that
this is not the plant mentioned in the Bible. It seems this may have
been marjoram, or the caper plant. It seems it may have been sor-
ghum or maidenhair spleenwort. Celsius devoted forty-two pages

to this discussion and considered eighteen different plants withou
coming to any conclusion, and ever since then the controversy ha
gained in documentation but not in clarification.

Manna invites similar speculation.

In the Bible pictures I looked at as a child, this feast, which
fell from heaven at such a propitious moment, looked like smal
puffballs, and since I knew what these were, it was easy to believe
the Children of Israel were able to gather a quick and more or less
sustaining breakfast. I do not find any reference to puffballs in
scholarly works. But it is pointed out that on the barren plains
and mountains of western Asia and northern Africa there are two
lichens (*Lecanora esculent* and *Lecanora affinis*) which can be
cooked and made into bread, and there is a similar one which
grows on the Sahara Desert and is gathered by the people there
and eaten in time of scarcity. Sometimes these lichens are lifted by
the wind and carried for great distances and fall almost like snow
upon places where they have never been known to grow. In 1854,
when there was famine in Persia, great showers of lichens fell like
the manna which whitened the wilderness, and these were grate-
fully gathered for food.

This explanation might seem to fill the requirements of the
text adequately, but there is still another. There is an alga (*Nos-
toc*) which grows in the tract where the Children of Israel wan-
dered hungrily, remembering "the fish which we did eat in Egypt
freely: the cucumbers and the melons, and the leeks and the
onions and the garlic." When there has been a heavy rainfall,
these algae multiply with incredible rapidity, and since they are
soft and gelatinous as soon as the sun comes up and dries the surface of the ground they disappear. This may have been the manna
which the Children of Israel "gathered every morning, every man
according to his eating: and when the sun waxed hot, it melted."

There is another plant which has intrigued every child who
has been told of the infant Moses being placed in a basket and

eft in the bulrushes by the river, to be discovered by Pharaoh's
aughter.

This tiny ark was woven from the stems of the papyrus plant
which was commonly used, and still is, to make baskets, cords,
andals and mats. But it had another and especial use, for it was
he basis of the earliest known paper. Its preparation was simple.
The stems were pared and the pith cut lengthwise on a flat
 board. Other slices were placed crosswise across these and the sur-
aces cemented by a sort of glue, and then put under heavy pres-
ure.

It may be noted that this is precisely the way plywood is
manufactured today, but there is another comparison not so immediately apparent. Moses, who was to receive the Ten Commandments indelibly engraved on stone, makes his first appearance in a
cradle of papyrus—the material which was to preserve man's earliest records written on paper.

The "reed shaken with the wind" was a different species and
was probably the very tall cane (*Arundo donax*) which grows
freely in many parts of Palestine and especially on the west side
of the Dead Sea. It sometimes reaches immense heights, with a
magnificent panicle of blossom on the top, but it is so slender and
pliant that when it has been flattened to the ground by a gust of
wind, it is so resilient it will rise again immediately to its former
erectness.

Plants with spiny growth are a characteristic of dry and desert
soil, and the briers and brambles, thorns, nettles and thistles which
plagued the Children of Israel when they tilled the soil, are doubtless plaguing their remote descendants today. Indeed, we do not
need to journey to Palestine, but no farther than through a short
cut to the nearest brier patch to understand feelingly why these
sharply prickled growths were used in the ancient prophecies of
doom as a threat of punishment of the wicked. Only when we are
disentangled from our immediate torment and a safe distance away

from it, can we enjoy the sonorous words of Isaiah, "And thorn shall come up in palaces, nettles and brambles in the fortresse thereof: and it shall be a habitation of dragons and court for owls.

Oddly enough, two of the plants which are usually though of as being the thorns of the Bible did not grow in the Holy Lan until recently. The crown-of-thorns (*Euphorbia splendens*) wa introduced from Madagascar and the prickly pear cactus (*Opun tia*) from America.

As for the trees and grains, fruits and vegetables, familiar t the Biblical folk four thousand years ago, and many of them fa miliar to us, these are beyond the scope of a book about gardens

When the etymologists and botanists forsake us—or we for sake them—then the folklorists pick us up.

In the Middle Ages, before Linnaeus' system of binomia nomenclature, hundreds of plants were named for the saints. There were St. Andrew's-cross (*Ascyrum hypericoides*), St. Augustine grass (*Stenotaphrum secundatum*), St. Bernard's-lily (*Anthericum liliago*), St. Brigid's anemone, St. Dabeoc's-heath (*Daboecia cantabrica*), St. James's-flower (*Lotus jacobaeus*), St. Joseph's-wand (*Pentstemon acuminatus*), St. Lucie cherry (*Prunus mahaleb*), to mention only a few. The St. John's-worts constitute the whole genus *Hypericum* and some of its species are popular in our own gardens.

Although we may have forgotten or have never known the origin of their names, we are not likely to neglect St. Patrick's shamrock, for the 17th of March finds it worn with patriotism or amusement, in this country quite as widely as in Ireland.

The legend has it that St. Patrick was preaching about the Trinity and found this theological tenet as difficult to explain to his congregation as has many a lesser preacher since. When he was questioned by some of the bolder ones as to how three persons could be one, the quick-witted saint leaned over and picked a clover leaf and, holding it up for them all to see, said, "Behold in

his trifoliate leaf how three Persons in the Godhead can exist, and
et be One." The illustration not only clarified the muddled situa-
on, but led to further amplification. Sometimes the stalk repre-
ented the path of life, with the right leaf for purgatory, the left
or Hades, and the middle one for heaven. It also became an em-
lem of faith, hope and charity, and was used in ecclesiastical
rnament and may be seen at the ends of crosses in church win-
ows.

The shamrock was not the only plant to be thus interpreted.
panish monks in South America called the *Passiflora* the *flos pas-
ionis* or passion-flower, and by it worked out the most ingenious
ymbolism to fix the story of the Crucifixion in the minds of their
imple followers. The lobed leaves were the hands of Christ's per-
ecutors, the tendrils the whips with which He was punished.
The sepals and petals were the ten disciples, although, for some
eason, Judas and Peter are not among them. In the pistil could be
seen the three nails and in the five stamens the five wounds. The
seed pod was the sponge dipped in vinegar, while the short stalk
below it represented the pillar at which Our Lord was scourged.
Opinions were divided about the fringed corona. Some interpreted
it as the nimbus which surrounded the sacred head and others as
the parted vestments and still others as the Crown of Thorns.
Neither was it forgotten that the number of filaments in the
corona is the same as the number of thorns in the crown.

Similar symbolism, although by no means so elaborate, was
traced in other flowers and fruits. Figs, when cut crosswise, show
a green cross on the white pulp, with five seeds for the five
wounds. In the Canary Islands, it is customary to cut bananas
lengthwise, because when sliced across they too reveal the symbol
of the Crucifixion.

These legends are Scriptural only as they refer to holy matters. And so are a hundred superstitions and names associated with
the Evil One. For the Devil has his advocates in the floral king-

dom, although these are no longer terrifying. While men are reluctant to give up their hope of heaven, their fear of hell seem comfortably lessening.

The garden leek, after having been dedicated to Jupiter an then to Thor, was finally handed over to the Devil, and with it large and mephitic family became an element in witchcraft. Who ever has shuddered over "Dracula" will remember the young gir who was bitten by a vampire. The resourceful doctor garlanded th window of her room with wild garlic and fastened a necklace of i around her throat to protect her from another attack, since vam pires, quite understandably, object to the horrid odor. Only when these protections were removed could the vampires lure her out side where, as I remember the story, they finally transformed he into one of themselves.

In spite of these malevolent implications, the leek managed to make the grade into respectability. It is the emblem of Wales and belongs to St. David, whose day is March the first.

A few of the old names like Devil's-horn (*Phallus im pudicus*) and Devil's-claw (*Ranunculus arvensis*) still linger in the English countryside, and in Mexico the prickly *Argemone mexi cana,* with its acrid yellow juice, is called Figo del Inferno, or the Devil's fig. Even we, who like to call *Artemisia abrotanum* old man, may not know the Old Man was originally a polite and cautious name for Satan himself.

These almost forgotten titles give the Evil One a very faint-hearted due. No one seems to feel very strongly any more about a devil with horns and claws. But there is still fervent and loving acknowledgment of the Blessed Virgin. Although the full title of Our Lady has been dropped from many flowers, she is recalled in scores of homely and reverent names, all of them sweeter for the implication.

For never, never, never has there been any deity, mythological or theological, any saint or sinner, any botanist or horticulturist, whose name has been associated with so many diverse flowers as the Virgin.

The whole month of May is Mary's month, and flowers past enumeration have been dedicated to her. There is such a multitude of them and each one has such a multitude of legends, that we will have quite enough if we confine ourselves to a quaint category which deals only with her personal adornment and habits. Scattered through old garden books are references to these, although there is the usual confusion and duplication and variation common to all colloquialisms.

The Madonna is in her Virgin's-bower (*Clematis*), reclining on our lady's-cushion (*Armeria*), considering what she will wear. She has, of course, lady's-slippers (*Cypripedium*), garters (*Phalaris*) and fine yellow laces for the slippers (*Dodder*). She has pretty silver-white lady's-smocks (*Cardamine pratensis*) and several blue mantles (*Alchemilla*), set so close with blossoms that hardly any green is visible. She must decide on her eardrops, for she has two pairs (*Fuchsia* and *Dicentra*). She has gloves (*Digitalis*) and a thimble (*Campanula*), to keep all these articles in order. For her lady's tresses (*Spiranthes cernua*) she has a comb (*Scandia pecten veneris*) and a looking-glass (*Specularia*). In her own basin (*Veneris labrum*) she can wash her hands (*Orchis*), her fingers (*Vitis*) and her thumb (*Polygonum persicaria*), and also her navel (*Cotyledon umbilicus*) and her nipple (*Lapsana*).

If she wishes to write a letter she can unlock her desk with our lady's keys (*Primula*) and use her seal (*Convallaria*), and find a stamp in any one of her purses (*Portulaca*).

When she steps outside into her garden, she will find every flower named for her—grasses and mints, ferns and thistles, heather and clover, to say nothing of marigolds, rosemarys, marguerites, lilies and roses.

With all these she can get along very nicely during the day. When she becomes our lady-of-the-night (*Brunsfelsia*), she can

put on her ruffled nightcap (*Campanula medium*), put out he
candlestick (*Primula*) and lie down to sleep, although all sh
seems to have to soften her slumbers is bedstraw (*Galium verum*)

I do not know if children in England and the United State
are able to recite all these articles as they did in more devout days
but in France and Germany and Scandinavia many of them are
still cozily recalled.

If we find our vocabularies a bit mixed up by these conflict-
ing and redundant terminologies, we can blame it on those of ou
predecessors who did not have proper respect for binomial nomenclature, but sauntered through the centuries calling flowers whatever they pleased or whatever pleased their fathers and mothers.

And if we are confronted by the proof—incontrovertible—
that our mental images of Biblical scenes are historically incon-
sistent, we can blame some of it on the painters.

For in the early days of the Church, the only acceptable matter for artists was the Bible, and those painters who depicted the
Holy Land, which they had never seen, illustrated it from models
which were near at hand. Botticelli's Virgin is crowned against a
background of Italian mountains and castles, and the Magi come
to Bethlehem across Italian bridges spanning Italian rivers. Man-
tegna's St. John receives his baptism kneeling on a floor of Carrara
marble in front of Renaissance columns. Grünewald sets forth the
stable of the Nativity with carved marble pillars and further furnished with statues on pedestals, with the concession of a few wisps
of hay sticking out of the raftered ceiling. Why should not the
Raphaelites use white Florentine lilies in their annunciations? Why
should not the pre-Raphaelites strew English daisies in the green of
English grass under the feet of the ass carrying Mother and Child
to Egypt?

They should and they did and their pictures are not less loved
because of this.

There are many Shakespeare gardens both in this country

and England in which only those flowers mentioned by Shake-speare are planted. He mentioned so many which are familiar to us today that such a garden looks quite like our own.

I do not happen to know any Bible gardens, but when I look out from Virginia windows, I see fig trees which very properly bear figs instead of thistles. I see tamarisk trees, with their long feathery branches veiled in spring by a gauze cloud of pink, and they seem to grow as well as they did in Beersheba and Gilead. That thick gourd vine over a new car port has apparently grown up as quickly as the one which sheltered Jonah, and if anyone wants to quibble that Jonah's vine was really the castor oil tree (*Ricinus communis*), we have these, too.

There are grape arbors and, as in the Song of Solomon, "the vines with tender grapes give a good smell." There are patches of yellow mustard. It is not the *Brassica nigra* which grows high enough for "the birds of the air to come and lodge in the branches thereof," but it is mustard, and if we had faith as a grain of one of its seeds we could move the Blue Ridge Mountains, assuming that this were desirable. There is the rose of Sharon and the lily-of-the-valley and we can, in a jiffy, gather a dish of herbs which, eaten in contentment, is a greater feast than beefsteak from the stalled ox, served in hatred.

In the autumn the locust tree clutters our yard ground with its dried pods, and recalls those which nourished St. John in the desert. There is a green bay tree and a holly tree, juniper and broom. A weeping willow hangs over a neighbor's little brook as it hung over the banks of the barada near Damascus.

In the spring, in Virginia, our grass is green and groweth up, but in the heat of summer it is, alas, too frequently dried brown and withered. If we are thrifty, we do not consume it by fire but trundle it to the compost heap. But in any case we cannot dodge the fact that all flesh is grass and all the goodliness thereof is as a flower of the field. There are red Turk's head lilies aplenty in our gardens, and anemones, too, if we prefer the latter arguments, and tall mallows which we hope we will not "for want and famine" have to cut up for food as did the poor people in Job's day.

We seem able to have a Biblical garden with no effort at all or even without realizing we have planted one.

As for the painters, if there are any today who are painting Bible scenes, I see no reason why they should confine their floral embellishments to specimens from stipulated geographical areas. The wreaths of the Flemish painters encircling sacred groups are glorious with Flemish roses and tulips, and if Franklin Watkins should do a similar wreath around his swirling angels, who would cavil if he used apple blossoms from Michigan, goldenrod from Alabama and roses from Portland, Oregon?

Such anachronisms are not confined to flowers. Murillo's Virgin is a soft Señora holding upright a little Son, not less Spanish for the nimbus around His head. Rembrandt's heavily sleeping baby in a Dutch cap, and the rigid blond infants of van der Weyden bear small resemblance to Perugino's chubby Italian boys. Rossetti's Virgin is a gentle English schoolgirl.

In a recent Christmas card from China, I noted that the Virgin and St. Joseph have almond eyes and are becomingly dressed in high-collared Chinese coats, while the smiling small boy between them has straight black bangs.

These things are quite as they should be.

We acknowledge the services of scholars in setting us right about the botany of ancient Palestine, Egypt and Arabia, but we acknowledge another debt to those who have passed along the floral legends of saints and sinners, and to those painters who gave us a Child, who, like the flowers which so often garland His pictures, belongs to every country and stretches out His hands to bless the world.

. . . the unicorn is subdued to gentleness at the sight of a virgin, and will come and lay his head in her lap, which is the only means by which he can be caught on account of his swiftness and ferocity.

AELIAN XVI, 20

ANIMALS IN THE GARDEN

Foxglove
DIGITALIS PURPUREA

The animals whose forms best decorate a garden are the animals we love best; in other words, our own pets and familiar companions.

When I see our herd of Siamese cats flash across the flower bed and swarm directly up the perpendicular garden wall and dispose themselves along the top in effective groups and attitudes, I consider it an exhibition of synchronized grace. When my neighbor's dog bounds over the same wall and lands on an iris or a poppy, I regard it as a clumsy and impertinent performance. Without doubt, my neighbor regards these acrobatics with reverse emotions, although she is too gentle to mention the business, to say nothing of being too well bred to take the world into her confidence as I am doing at this moment.

Any dispassionate observer could hardly fail to note that cats scratch up newly spaded patches and patches newly seeded. They cannot resist a freshly dug hole but must immediately go for it with vigor and set the earth flying. They roll over the spears of the sprouting fraxinellas, biff the swaying racemes of the bleeding-heart, chase rose petals, make love among the lilies and go to sleep in the pansy border. They are usually amusing, sometimes infuriating and always decorative. I do not happen to know a dog, no matter how rambunctious, who can match in destructiveness any pussy, no matter how meek.

Nevertheless our cats—not anyone else's cats but ours—seem to me to enhance, to enliven, to embellish my flower beds and borders with an effect otherwise unattainable.

I venture to suggest that most people are similarly biased when it comes to the question of animals in the garden. Josephine Gibson Knowlton wrote a unique book about turtles. Characteristically, it is called *My Turtles*. In it she describes in lovingest detail their habits gustatory, ambulatory and amorous. She relates their leisurely and toothless antics. She absorbedly tabulates their names and sizes and the various colors and patterns of their shells. She calculates their ages, and gives amazing photographs of them sitting and standing, opening doors, sharing meals, begging for food and mating.

Unsusceptible, indeed, must be the reader who, by the time he is halfway through this absurd and affectionate herpetological account, does not agree with Mrs. Knowlton that a turtle is one animal whose association with a garden is unflawed by mischief, and who furnishes blameless amusement to his human master or mistress without demanding a single thing in return.

Probably the owners of peacocks, spreading their iridescent trains across meticulously tended greensward, see only the glory of their plumage and never hear the discordance of their screechings. The Japanese make pets of crickets and keep them in dainty cages, while the Chinese train frogs to croak at the signal of a bamboo whistle. Yan Kuei's white parrot with coral feet was buried in a ilver coffin in the heart of the Emperor's garden. As for carp, hose Orientals who seem always to have had plenty of time, think a lifetime not misspent in breeding these to extravagant colors— gold, mauve, silver, speckled, black—and to grotesque forms with multiple diaphanous fins and bulgy eyes. Priests, literary men and gentlemen of fashion cultivated exotic goldfish as they cultivated flowers, fed them by hand and called each one by name.

A goat, of course, cannot logically be associated with a garden, for these agile creatures who gave us the word capricious and illustrate it in every leap, can turn a green spot into a barren one in the brief time it takes to crop it. Apparently they have no resentment at being barred from too intimate domestic areas. In fact, one of the cheerfulest goats I ever saw was balanced on a horrent slope of lava in Hawaii, munching with relish an excessively prickly cactus.

But if the goat cannot qualify as an animal who belongs in a garden, surely we can include, if only indirectly, the tiny-footed, sure-footed, velvet-eared donkey. For how could the hillside gardens of Italy have been created without the patient little burden-bearer who carried the stones away in wicker panniers and brought back the fertile earth to unfertile spots? It is the fashion—it has been the fashion for centuries—to ridicule this neatly formed and softly tinted creature. It has been overloaded, lashed, galled, lamed, tormented and generally abused by owners more brutal than any brute, and one often sees it starting sorrowfully upon a cruel task with great tears rolling down its cheeks.

And yet, what would the old Italian painters have done without the ass to carry the tired Virgin to Bethlehem, without an ass to bear Her and the Holy Babe away from the wrath of Herod? And what animal did our Lord choose on the day of His triumphal entry into Jerusalem? He chose a donkey to ride upon and to share His brief acclaim. Around the long gray ears, which always before and ever since have been derided, there swirled the sweet hosannas of praise, and on the road were spread green palm branches, so that the small hooves might step softly.

Certain animals staunchly maintain their allotted positions in the gardens of the saints. There was the lion who shared the exile of St. Jerome on his rocky hillside. According to some of the painters, this companionable creature was the size of a large cat, with a bland expression and tremendous mustache. According to others, he approximated a small elephant, with a mane neatly curled in poodle dog fashion. Sometimes this anomalous form is worked out in careful detail, standing on guard atop a rock. Sometimes all that is visible is his plaintive face, peering out of the cave. But wherever the good saint Jerome is, there is the lion, and he is always brown, to match the tanned skin of his human friend.

And there are all the birds which gathered around St. Francis as he stood in his own garden in Assisi and which have been gathering ever since around statues of him in gardens all over the world.

When we come to statues of animals in gardens, we find them a legion. Of course, there are dolphins supporting fountains, and satyrs and fauns and centaurs placed at the end of a vista, although it may be debated if these latter were predominantly animal or human. At all events, they owe their singularity to their former rather than their latter attributes.

On the other hand, the bacchantes and mermaids, elves and cupids, in marble or in lead or in bronze or in ceramics, are notable for their human characteristics, while Pan—a favorite subject in garden sculpture—differs from them all in being part god and part goat.

The iron stag which once stood at bay in simulated and emasculated alertness seems, like the American bison, on the road to extinction. So are most of the marble lions which were wont to stretch themselves on the top of stairs leading down to some majestic garden. The majestic gardens themselves give indication of following them to oblivion. For while we are continually being told that our standard of living is rising, it is impossible to deny that our gardens are becoming less regal.

The man who guides his power-mower over his own lawn is supposed to enjoy greater ease, leisure and enlightenment than his grandfather who hired a laborer to do the job. However, the man who cuts his own grass is not usually tempted to commission a sculptor to model him a pair of marble lions. Our standard of living may indeed be higher than ever before, but paradoxically the famous lawns of England were created and maintained in their perfection not only before the power-mower, but before any lawn-mower at all. These were the lawns which offered appropriate settings to marble lions, dolphin fountains and strutting peacocks.

Perhaps some of the oldest, and certainly some of the loveliest, gardens ever wrought by hands, and still existing, are those which bloom in the tapestries of the fourteenth and fifteenth centuries. It was at this time that "The Pattern of a Thousand Flowers" was carefully worked out for such wall hangings. A thousand flowers, and not one too many.

In 1947, many thousands of Americans went to the exhibitions of French tapestries which were loaned to the United States by the French government, and many of them saw for the first time these medieval gardens of silk and wool. They saw borders of flowering pinks and poppies, foxgloves and heartsease and English daisies, meticulously accurate or poetically stylized, all blooming together from a ground of blue or tan or green. Over and among these familiar flowers frolicked squirrels and crickets and rabbits, storks, horses, owls, falcons and peacocks. Neither were the legendary animals lacking for, wrought into the floral design, were winged stags, dragons and seven-headed beasts.

Such deep borders framed virgins, saints and martyrs, kings and hunters. They framed temples, pavilions, parks, palaces and chariots, bridges and waterfalls.

Perhaps the tapestries which charmed the greatest number of visitors was the famous set of six, entitled "The Lady with the Unicorn." In all of them the Lady, flanked by a lion, the symbol of bravery, and the unicorn, a symbol of purity, stands on a deep blue island against a rose-red background. There is no sky—the background, like the foreground, is a field of flowers. There are architectural features—columns, loggias, steps; there is garden furniture —tables, stools, cushions and musical instruments. But the allegory concerns the senses, and these are symbolized by the Lady and by the animals so closely surrounding her.

In one such celestial-earthly scene representing "Sight," the Lady is seated, holding up a mirror. A unicorn stands with two dainty hooves on her lap and peers into the burnished glass from which peers forth a tiny replica of himself.

"Hearing" is symbolized by the Lady standing and playing on a portable organ, set on a table covered with a rich cloth and placed among the flowers. An attendant works the bellows and the animals around her listen intently.

For the sense of "Smell" the Lady has taken a chaplet of flowers from a tray held by a servant. Behind her a monkey on a stool imitatively sniffs the blossoms in a basket.

In "Taste" she picks, with her right hand, a sweetmeat from a golden compote, while on her left hand perches a parakeet, beating its tiny brilliant wings.

Most affecting of all is the portrayal of "Touch." Here, while the Lady tenderly strokes the horns of the unicorn, in the background a wistfully watching little brown monkey fingers his chains.

The sixth tapestry is not part of the allegorical series, although the same Lady and the animals appear in it. In this she is standing before a tent around the top of which appear the words "A Mon Seul Désir." As she selects jewels from a casket held by an attendant, the lion holds back one flap of the tent and the unicorn the other. At her right, on a cushion, is her poodle.

In these six ineffable tapestries the reality and the symbolism are so merged that while we recognize each animal and flower it seems entirely proper that fruits and flowers appear at the same time on the same tree, that the jeweled birds do not destroy the jeweled berries, and that lions and unicorns sit on fragile blossoms without crushing them. Here is the perfect garden, stretching unbrokenly from our feet into heaven.

This is the garden which is profoundly moving to those who carry the theory of immortality to its ultimate conclusion—that the souls not only of people but of animals persist through the cycle of change named death. Thus, in heaven, they hope they may find the dear faces of flowers which they loved on earth, and may meet again those animals who, with them, delighted in a garden, and still continue in that delight.

Surely this is the Paradise William Blake envisioned when he writes of the lion in his splendor and strength walking around the fold of defenseless sheep and suddenly pitying their tender cries, and feeling the golden tears of divine compassion flowing from his eyes.

This Paradise, where the strong protect the weak instead of preying upon them, is, of course, the one toward which man is approaching—not the one he left, clad in a fig leaf.

It is not strange that the Paradise at the beginning of life, like the one beyond life, is in all religions and in all regions and climates pictured as a garden. And in the gardens there are always animals.

Remember that serpent?

A Duet.

"Flowers nodding gaily, scent in air,
Flowers posied, flowers for the hair,
Sleepy flowers, flowers bold to stare—"
        "O pick me some!"

"Shells with lip, or tooth, or bleeding gum,
Tell-tale shells, and shells that whisper *Come,*
Shells that stammer, blush, and yet are dumb—"
        "O let me hear!"

"Eyes so black they draw one trembling near,
Brown eyes, caverns flooded with a tear,
Cloudless eyes, blue eyes so windy clear—"
        "O look at me!"

"Kisses sadly blown across the sea,
Darkling kisses fair and free,
Bob-a-cherry kisses 'neath a tree—"
        "O give me one!"
Thus sang a king and queen in Babylon.

                              T. STURGE MOORE

From *Collected Poems of T. Sturge Moore.* By permission of The Macmillan
Company, publishers.

GARDENS IN THE AIR

Orchid

CATTLEYA HARDYANA

The hanging gardens of Babylon still have power by their very name to tease the imagination. We think of them as vaguely suspended and floating in the air, and the word "pensile," which is often used in describing them, further emphasizes the image of something pendant and swaying. As a matter of fact, they were planted on an extraordinarily solid foundation. But they are none the less fascinating on account of this.

Nebuchadnezzar, who was King of Babylon about five centuries before Christ, married "a wife he was fond of, out of one of the Provinces." This was the mountainous Province of Media, and the lady, whose name was Amytis, found the flat plain of Babylon and the confining walls of the palace not at all to her liking. To gratify her homesick longing for high places and cool breezes, her husband constructed the gardens which were one of the seven wonders of the ancient world.

These consisted of arched vaults which were built one after

another on checkered, cubelike foundations. There were passages under the arches, and the pillars which supported them were of baked brick and asphalt. Furthermore, these pillars were hollow, and contained sufficient earth for the trees which were planted on the terraces above to send their roots to the ground and get nourishment and support. The terraces, which were high above the city, were reached by a stairway and beside this ran a screw, up which a force of men was constantly employed to pump water from the Euphrates.

On this cool and dust-free elevation were planted fruit trees and many kinds of flowers, so that they became "at least the most airy gardens as well as the most costly that have been heard of in the world."

They may have been the most airy and the most costly, but they were not the only hanging gardens, for Semiramis, the half-legendary Assyrian princess, was so taken by the idea that whenever she conquered a Province—which she did frequently—she had constructed in it a similar hanging garden.

Nebuchadnezzar was a tremendous builder. There are many descriptions of his palaces, constructed of bright yellow bricks cemented with fine white lime mortar. On their walls were large bas-reliefs in bright blue paste; the floors were of white and mottled sandstone, and the courtyards were paved with limestone and black basalt, and at their entrances were gigantic basalt lions. These palaces were encircled by a high wall in which were one hundred gates, of cedar and copper. It was wide enough for a four-horse chariot to turn around on its top and was protected by a moat and lagoons. Where it was visible from the palace, it was surfaced with glazed and enameled bricks of brilliant colors.

The King was so proud of these architectural achievements of his that he described them at length, and the description is still preserved in cuneiform inscriptions.

But such ambition and vainglorious pleasure in earthly possessions was his undoing. He was banished from his throne and made to dwell with the beasts of the field, to eat grass, to be wet with the dews, until his hair grew as long as an eagle's feathers and his nails like birds' claws. When his punishment was completed and he humbly acknowledged that the King of Heaven was greater than he, his majesty and his possessions were restored to him. The cuneiform inscriptions make no mention of this humiliating period in the life of one of the greatest monarchs of antiquity, but it is related with relish in the Book of Daniel.

Since Nebuchadnezzar, a good many men have built terraced gardens for their wives' pleasure or for their own prideful ambitions. Modern zoning laws, which require setbacks in the upper stories of tall buildings in cities, provide spaces which are more and more often being converted into penthouse gardens.

These are faced with problems unknown to Nebuchadnezzar and Amytis. Their hanging garden did not have to be very high to overlook the low-spread city and level plain. It caught the breeze and escaped the dust, and there were always those slaves whose only and continuous task was to pump the river water up to the higher level of the terrace to cool the air and irrigate the trees and shrubs and flowers.

Our penthouse gardens are swept by currents and cross-currents of high velocity created by the architecture of the surrounding buildings. Windbreaks of specially processed glass or sturdy lattices are necessary, and awnings and umbrellas must be anchored with exceptional firmness. Dust and soot settle on the leaves and flowers, on the grass and gravel and on the furniture. Irrigation may be a laborious and costly business. Unshaded winter sun may do as much damage as summer storms.

Notwithstanding these difficulties, there are more and more penthouse gardens every year, giving pleasure to their owners and their guests. Smooth-leaved plants, from which soot and dust can be readily washed, hardy growers such as privet, ailanthus and wisteria, and blooming plants in pots, which can be moved or re-placed, serve very well for greenery. Awnings, trellises and outdoor furniture, and perhaps a small fountain, complete the effect. When the soil is deep enough and rich enough and the windbreaks high enough, there can be a very pleasant succession of bloom hundreds of feet above the city thoroughfare.

Whoever is interested in having a penthouse or terraced garden can do no better than to read *Your Garden in the City* by Natalie Gomez. Here is sound instruction about structural weights, drainage, soil, and the choice of shrubs, vines, flowers and herbs, and information as to how to spray, prune, water and nourish them.

The fascination of such gardens—as it was with those of Amytis two thousand years ago—is the ever surprising novelty they offer of walking on turf and picking flowers ten or twenty stories above the heads of passers-by.

Equally delightful may be the reverse—the sunken garden: for, looking down on flowers below where we are standing is en-tirely different from seeing them on a level. We find this again when the prettiest view of a bed or border is from an upper win-dow, and frequently this is the most advantageous place to study its pattern and plan its rearrangement. Le Nôtre, laying out the parterres of Versailles, admitted that the best view of them would be enjoyed by the governesses living in the garrets.

Gardens planted in different levels and with varying perspec-tives have great individuality. An abrupt cliff or steep hillside holds up its drifts and masses like a gigantic tilted palette. A ledge two or three feet wide, and running knee high or shoulder high along a wall, offers a space for a border in which the flowers are nearer the eyes and which, incidentally, can be worked not on the weary knees, but standing in elegant erectness—or even sitting.

There are certain cities which one always remembers en-veloped in cloudlike streamers of color. Victoria, in British Columbia, is such a city, where swaying bouquets planted in baskets affixed high on the corner street posts raise coral, lavender, gold and blue up into the sky, while their greenery floats below and their sweetness perfumes the air.

These are truly hanging gardens in miniature.

Window boxes, inside and out, pots of plants on glass shelves against a window—these familiar arrangements owe a great deal of their charm to the fact that they are not on a level with our feet, but nearer our eyes and noses.

Do wallflowers, or a clump of flowering sedum, ever look so delightful as when they have seeded themselves and are thriftily blooming on the thatched or turfed roof of a low cottage?

Does a mimosa ever smell so sweet as when it holds out a branch of its scented silky heads just below the window of an upper bedroom? Or a forsythia, when it pours its golden bells down from the top of a wall or a bank?

One reason magnolia blossoms are so breath-taking in their generous and immaculate unfolding is because we see them against the sky.

And what about those showy flowers which bloom high above the earth and need no soil whatsoever to nourish them, but only heat, light and moisture?

The tree-perching orchids are truly flowers of the air and, if we can imagine a Colombian jungle of trees growing around the hanging gardens of Babylon, we can imagine Nebuchadnezzar and Amytis stepping over to the edge of their terrace and picking Cattleyas from the forks of their topmost branches.

There are orchids in our temperate zone which are among the most prized wild flowers—lady's-slippers, swamp pinks, moccasin flowers, arethusa, ladies' tresses, coral root. More than forty Orchidaceae are found in every one of our States from Illinois to New York, and more are to be discovered. These, however, are terrestrial, thrusting their roots into bogs, sandy plains, and into cool damp meadows. In Australia there are two species that grow and blossom underground, and orchids have been found blooming even within the Arctic Circle. Those which are sold by florists, their stems bound in gold or silver foil and a rosette of ribbons under their chins, are tree perchers (epiphytes). In their natural state they grow in the moss or debris in the fork of a tall tree, and are most abundant in tropical climates at an elevation of four to six thousand feet.

They are often carelessly called parasites, but this is entirely incorrect, for they do not feed upon the tree but use it merely for a support. They can flourish clinging to a piece of bark or a plank nailed on a wall or even on the bare wall itself.

Those which are cultivated in commercial greenhouses are usually potted for convenience, but the pots do not contain soil but a special spongy peat made from fern roots (*Osmunda*). The roots frequently wrap themselves outside the pots and push down through the slats of the platform to dangle below like the untied threads of a raveled weaving.

In tropical countries anyone can have a collection of orchids growing on the walls of his patio and needing merely a bit of roughened surface to cling to. The vanilla vine is a climbing orchid, bearing forty or fifty beans in a year which, before the production of synthetic vanillin, were the source of our flavoring extract.

Those which are made into fashionable corsages have been brought to amazing variety by years of cultivation and hybridization. Some resemble pansies; some spider webs. The professional orchid grower combines his pollens with greatest care, even wearing a sterilized mask when he handles them. It takes about ten months for the seeds to germinate in a prepared solution in cotton-plugged containers, and then the non-viable ones, which are transparent, must be culled from the viable ones, which are opaque. A clump of the minute seedlings is then planted in a small pot and, after a year, these are separated into tiny plants and each one is individually potted. After another year, these are again transplanted into still larger pots, and so on, until after five or six years the mature plant, with its thick stiff leaves, bears blossoms—lavender, rose, yellow, mustard, purest white—streaked, splotched, dotted or clear—immense or miniature, to meet the market requirements.

If it takes a long time to bring an orchid to the age when it will bear its yearly blossom—although some hybrids flower oftener—that blossom makes up for it by its long life. A Cattleya, when cut, may last two weeks, and when on the tree be fresh for a month. As for the plant itself, it may live for forty or fifty years. And if each bloom brings a handsome price, certain plants are worth hundreds and even thousands of dollars.

This painstaking scientific cultivation is not all. Every so often the plants must be refreshed with wild jungle stock, and the searching for these aerial clumps in the high regions of South America, Siam, India and Malaya is an adventure and a business. Whoever wants a rattling good account of one such expedition can find it in a book by Norman MacDonald called *The Orchid Hunters*.

It is possible for the amateur to raise orchids in a home greenhouse, in a sun parlor, or even in a terrarium. When suspended in the air, with their roots exposed to light and heat and moisture, the plants with their rigid leaves and their swollen bases for storing water and their rare bursts of bloom are an exotic accent amid more familiar flowers.

Another epiphyte which would have commended itself to our royal pair in Babylon is Spanish moss, or long moss, which drapes the trees in gray floating veils—especially live oaks and cypresses—in southern United States. This does not belong to the orchid but to the pineapple family (*Bromeliaceae*) and neither is it a moss at all. In Florida, other epiphytes (*Tillandsia*), just to prove their independence of earth, dot themselves like rosettes along the telegraph wires.

While such skyey plants are too inaccessible for ordinary pedestrian enjoyment, almost any flower is enhanced when we can see it directly.

It is customary in the Scandinavian countries to have the sills of the principal windows wide enough to hold quite elaborate floral settings. Here is no mere stereotyped row of house plants, but thoughtful, and frequently extremely beautiful, arrangements of cut flowers or growing plants, accented by a piece of statuary, or fine porcelain, glass or silver.

Since such windows are frequently large corner ones, they give opportunity for varied effects and ingenuity.

Such a window might have at the two ends and in the exact center, small fan-shaped or circular lattices on which are trained ivy or wandering Jew. These vines, and others, may be twined into garlands against the white curtains or looped across the glass. Between them may be white and green china jardinières holding white cyclamen. Sparkling copper pots of salmon geraniums are grouped around a splendid ancient copper candlestick with a candle of precisely the same color as the geraniums. There are as many types of windowsill compositions as there are windows, and some of them are as pleasing as florist display windows worked out by professional decorators. In fact, they are frequently more pleasing, for they must be placed so that they are effective both from the room and the street and, like the daisy, must be lovely on both sides. These splashes of color give softness, and the graceful compositions give great interest to the otherwise non-committal façades of apartment houses.

Sometimes in a humble street or obscure alley there will be a basement window on the level of the sidewalk. The window is small; it may be the only one in a poor chamber. But the glass is clean and the white cotton curtains neatly ironed. On the sill in an old china sugar bowl is a four-inch cactus and beside it a little japanned tray—the best, perhaps the only treasure of the occupant of the room and shared by her with every passer-by.

In balconies in tropical lands flaming poinsettias sprawl out of tin cans. With oleanders in tubs, a bird in a cage and orchids any old where, it seems impossible that there should be room left for mamma to lean back in a chair, fanning herself, and for papa to sit beside her smoking and for a few naked babies to stick tiny brown arms and legs through the railings. On a fiesta day a gaudy shawl, or even a tablecloth or a bedspread, are hung out from this airy perch, for additional gaiety.

Percé, in Quebec, is a great natural rock garden thrusting out into the sea, slanting up into Mt. St. Anne, where it is accessible on only one side. Wherever you look, you must look up or look down. These sharply opposing elevations give the place its drama and endow the commonest wild flower with specialness. A buttercup on a path above your head is quite different from one on a path below. Indeed, you see the underneath of the flower in the former case and look down into its face in the latter.

Sometimes in old books we happen upon the words "the quarrel of a window." This was a lozenge-pane made crisscross to frame a section of out-of-doors. Through it one could study one's garden and the weather with confined concentration.

We do not have quarrels in our windows today, but many of us have discovered that if a mirror is hung in a room, so that it reflects the garden, it reveals hitherto unglimpsed possibilities of planting and transplanting. Painters sometimes use a mirror to study a scene in reverse, and they also use sets of right angles as an improvised frame without a mirror to confine selected portions.

When I was little, I took greatest delight in a Claude Lorraine mirror, which was kept handily on the table. It was almost black, in a black velvet case about four or five inches square. When it was held up in such a way as to catch a land or sea or sky scape, you saw a complete picture, small and intensified. We were told that Claude Lorraine, the French painter, had invented this to aid him in his landscape work, and I always remember it when I see one of his dark-toned pictures, although I now understand that this characteristic effect of his came not so much from copying the little reflected scene as by his use of underpainting in umber before applying the glazed color on top.

The Claude Lorraine mirror was in popular demand once upon a time by young ladies who dabbled in water colors as a polite accomplishment. In a small English churchyard there is a grave commemorating one of these, and under her name and the dates of her birth and death, her distinctions are listed as follows: "She was tall, blond, and passionate, but she painted well in water colors and was the second cousin of the Earl of Cork."

Gardeners instinctively follow the painter's trick of cocking a head first on one side and then on the other in studying an effect, although I am again informed that it is only amateur painters who do this. But the practice of turning a picture upside down to observe its design unobscured by representational elements is regrettably impossible with a garden. We cannot hold it upside down to study it and by the time we are old enough to become real gardeners we are too old to stand on our heads. The nearest we can get to it is when we are weeding with our faces almost to our feet and thus manage to obtain a passable reverse of our handiwork.

There have been many kinds of hanging gardens since Nebuchadnezzar built the first for Amytis but, like most garden lovers, these two prefer to stay—nicely carved in bas-relief—in their own.

The garden looks out over the high wall with its hundred gates to the Euphrates and beyond to the fields of wheat and groves of palm trees. Beyond these the brown desert stretches away to the horizon.

The royal couple sit at a table while an attendant stands beside them, offering a dish of fruit. All three of them are small as to waist and high as to shoulders and, furthermore, they have the peculiarity common in 500 B.C. of each having only half a face. They must always look directly at one another. Should they turn to look out over the garden, they must stand one behind the other, and continue to show their profiles.

However, one grows accustomed to everything. Nebuchadnezzar apparently loved Amytis as much as if she had had a whole face. And she probably admired the way he wore his black beard in tight braids.

At any rate, although no one knows precisely which palace or building the hanging gardens hung from, without question they existed and still exist in fine angular relief, while the King and Queen enjoy in perpetuity their fruits and flowers of stone.

Lavender, sweet-briar, orris. Here
Shall Beauty make her pomander,
Her sweet-balls for to lay in clothes
That wrap her as the leaves the rose.

Take roses red and lilies white,
A kitchen garden's my delight;
Its gillyflowers and phlox and cloves,
And its tall cote of irised doves.

KATHERINE TYNAN

And because the breath of flowers is far sweeter in the
air (where it comes and goes, like the warbling of
music) than in the hand, therefore nothing is more
fit for that delight than to know what be the flowers
and plants that do best perfume the air.

SIR FRANCIS BACON

From *Collected Poems of Katherine Tynan.* By permission of The Macmillan
Company, publishers.

THE INVISIBLE DIMENSION

Sweetbrier

ROSA EGLANTERIA,

It is sometimes embarrassing that a garden is such an unbribable character witness to whoever planned and tended it.

Our good taste, innate or acquired; our ignorance or experience; our energy or indolence are plainly set forth in our gardens, and no last minute setting to rights will disguise habitual disorder and no hasty camouflage of purchased potted plants in June will make up for procrastination with seeds and slips in April and May.

The most cursory visitor can see if we have balance and symmetry or are one of those who are deluded into thinking that a casual effect is obtained by carelessness. It is obvious whether we prefer rich deep colors or pastels, whether we appreciate the texture and form of foliage as well as of flowers, and whether we have the fortitude to attempt the more difficult summer garden as well as the easier ones of spring and fall.

Not so obvious is that invisible dimension which imparts to each garden its intangible and permeating quality—its fragrance.

The sense of smell in present-day human beings is vestigial.

We have merely to compare our olfactories with those of any normal animal to realize how faint and blurred ours have become since those ages when primitive man depended upon his nose to warn him of danger and guide him to his destination or his quarry. However, happily most of us have enough left to yield a peculiar pleasure—perhaps we may say pleasures, since through this fifth sense others are intensified.

It is a commonplace that there are only four fundamental tastes—sweet and sour, bitter and salty—and that all the rest of our gustatory savors and flavors depend upon our sense of smell.

Even more remarkable is the power of odors to touch and quicken our memories, so that sights and sounds, words and emotions, entirely forgotten, are, with a sudden and unexpected scent, simultaneously and poignantly revived.

Proust held a tisane in his hand, and in the split second that it took for the aroma to rise from the cup to his nostrils, he saw the whole town of Combray as he had known it long ago. He saw the houses and the church and the statues. He felt beneath his feet the pavement of the suburbs which surrounded the city. He heard the people talking in the streets and the children calling in the gardens. He smelled the flowers and noted the trees. It all came back in its entirety and in such acute detail that he needed four and a half rushing pages to write it down.

Few of us, fortunately for the world, have such hypersensitivity as Proust. But a good many of us, fortunately for ourselves, have retained a sufficiently keen sense of smell to distinguish and delight in the myriad fragrances of the garden.

Nurserymen's catalogues, those tours de force of prose and photography, limp painfully in analyzing flowery fragrances, perhaps because accurate description of odors evades even those virtuosi of untrammeled rhetoric. About the best they or anyone else can do is describe an odor in the term of some other sense, such as sharp or shrill or heavy. Or, an even franker admission of indequacy, to describe one odor in terms of another, such as saying pink is spicy, a lily smells like a lemon, one of the candytufts smells like some of the hyacinths and the leaves of one of the geraniums smell like a rose. Perhaps Gertrude Stein really meant something when she said a rose is a rose is a rose.

While there has never been any specific vocabulary for odors, there has been a device for classifying them with precision. This was the odophone invented by Septimus Piesse, and based upon the theory that there is a gamut among odors similar to that among sounds. He drew two clefs—a treble and a bass—and, taking about fifty odors, he arranged them on the clefs, taking the sharp smells to correspond with the high notes and the heavy smells with the low notes. For example, the note E (fourth space in the treble clef) corresponds with orange (called Portugal). D (first space below clef) corresponds with violet, and F (fourth space above clef) with ambergris. In the bass clef, patchouly is C (sixth space below) and rose is on the first line above. A proper bouquet of odors should be like notes in a musical chord. One false note can destroy the harmony.

The inventor of this odophone—George William Septimus Piesse (1820–1882)—was an Englishman who made a life study and wrote books about the art of perfumery. He believed that the sense of smell is a gift comparable in value to any of the other four senses; that it not only protects us from dangers but that its development can give us unique and exquisite pleasure, beneficial to both mind and body. Since he himself could instantly distinguish and name several hundred different odors, he was obviously fitted to work out his odophone and, while he chose only those odors which are especially used in perfumery, he believed there was no odor to which he could not assign its corresponding key. Incidentally, he remarks that as a rule young people prefer heavy odors and older people lighter ones.

I do not know whether professional perfumers use Piesse's

odophone, but I do know that his book, *The Art of Perfumery*, has gone through many editions and was brought up to date as late as 1935. To read it is like opening the gate into a country which most of us never knew existed, but which we will be conscious of for the rest of our lives.

To be sure, we may not want to bother with an odophone chart, but the knowledge that such a law as it sets forth is logical may help us to use more discrimination in combining flowers both in the garden and in vases—not mingling lilacs and lily-of-the-valley, or gardenias and tuberoses.

Despite the lack of a vocabulary for odors, there is no lack of sweet-scented flowers themselves.

Each of the three flowering seasons is a strand in the perfumed braid which crowns the year.

There is the strand of spring when everything, including the earth itself, smells sweet. Trailing arbutus, hyacinth, poet's narcissus, violets, lily-of-the-valley—the very syllables of their names are redolent of spring.

There is the strand of summer, with roses and peonies, the pinks, the lilies, phlox and sweet peas.

There is the strand of autumn, with the aroma of chrysanthemums and marigolds and, if their flowers have been kept cut, wallflowers and mignonette. With the first light touch of frost, the heliotrope gushes its final and finest fragrance.

All of these and many, many more are accompanied by a similar array of shrubs: lilacs, gardenias, mock-orange; and of vines: honeysuckle, wisteria and clematis.

With such an array it would seem that scent is an integral quality in every flower and that any garden must smell delicious. But, as a matter of fact, there are some scents so fugitive that only keen noses can enjoy them, such as the earthy aroma of daffodil petals when crushed between the fingers, and the tips of young lilac leaves.

There are some flowers, like the camellia, which have no odor, and there are others with a noxious stench.

The trillium is like a pretty girl who should use a deodorant and doesn't, and the male ailanthus is a dreadful example of BO, thereby gaining the graphic name of stinkwood. Since the female is spared this misfortune, it more properly qualifies for the title tree of heaven. John Clare speaks of the henbane's "sickly stinking bloom." The mayapple is disagreeably scented, and so is cleome and so are some of the orchids. However, the worst offender is the tropical *Amorphophallus*. This vile body shoots up from a bulbous root stock with amazing speed. The stalk, which may be three or four feet high, is dark colored and bears a single gigantic spathe and a red spadix two feet long. The inflorescence is an ugly liver color, but not so ugly as the smell, which rivals that of a dead horse. *Amorphophallus rivieri* is sometimes grown as an unsavory curiosity, but is in no danger of becoming a garden favorite. Neither is the *Titanum* of the same family. The gigantic herb, which is native to East India, was seen for the first time in America when it bloomed in the New York Botanical Garden, in 1937. Its spathe was four feet across, bell-shaped and highly colored, and reeked of the effluvia of drains and all corruption.

After these two so rankly and frankly foul examples, it seems rather finicky to object to bugbane and datura, or to complain about the pungency of marigolds.

Some flowers come in both scented and unscented varieties, such as violets, columbine, iris and even heliotrope.

Some are sweet when the air is damp and some when the sun is hot. Others, like nicotiana, fraxinella, bouncing bet, night-scented stock and evening primrose, give their fragrance best after dark. *Silene vespertina* is fragrant in the early morning as well as in the evening.

With some, it is not the flower but the leaves which are aromatic, as with balms, mints, lemon verbena and certain geraniums. Some flowers, like lavender, hold their fragrance and their flavor, after they are dried. Some have a different scent by day and by night.

Any garden encyclopedia lists such perennials and annuals, according to season, and gives the most suitable climate and conditions for their culture.

The use of perfumes and the art—nowadays the business—of mixing them is older than recorded history. They were part of the ceremonials of life of Nineveh and Assyria; of ancient Persia, Babylonia and Arabia; of India, China and Tibet.

In the tombs of ancient Egyptians are found exquisite perfume containers. The Pharaohs are carved or painted holding a burning censer in one hand and casting pastilles into it with the other. Six centuries before Christ, the Chinese poet Li Tai-po dipped his writing brushes in ink scented with larkspur.

Later, the Greeks and Romans were lavish with their use of perfume. Nero burned more incense on his wife's funeral pyre than all Arabia could produce in a year. When Plotius Plancus, a political exile from Rome, was in hiding, the wind caught the scent of the perfume which he always used and betrayed him to his pursuers.

It has seemed of sufficient importance for historians to record that Socrates disapproved of all perfumes. "When both are scented you cannot tell a gentleman from a slave," he said. Casanova did not hesitate to heighten his fascination with perfumes, while Beau Brummell, on the other hand, declared that no man of fashion should be scented, but should send his linen to be washed and dried on Hampstead Heath.

History is equally detailed when it comes to the ladies. Queen Elizabeth had a particularly acute sense of smell, and the *Lives of the Queens of England* records that perfumes were never richer, more elaborate or more costly than during her reign. She had a cloak of perfumed Spanish leather, and her shoes and her gloves were perfumed. Many pomanders were presented to her as New Year's gifts and among the list is the somewhat puzzling item of "A farye girdle of pomander." The pomander was a little ball of perfumed paste carried in the pocket or worn around the neck. Later, these were slipped into exquisite pieces of jewelry cunningly made to contain them.

Another celebrated lady, Medea, owed her power of magic to her skill as a perfumer and her invention of warm vapor baths. She used her bath fomentations secretly, claiming they made men active and improved their health. Since her apparatus consisted of a caldron, wood and a fire, it was believed her clients were boiled. Poor old Pelias died in such a caldron.

Cleopatra carried her sachets with her jewels to her sepulchre.

As for the Empress Josephine, she was so inordinately fond of musk that, despite Napoleon's remonstrances, the very walls of her dressing room at Malmaison became impregnated with it. Legend has it that forty years after her death the strong scent persisted, in spite of scrubbing and even repainting.

Perfumes were enjoyed not only for their own sake, but because they neutralized or disguised other odors.

In those bad old days which are sometimes called the good old days, and which lasted until comparatively recently, strong perfumes were necessary to drown the disagreeable odors of unwashed bodies. Incenses were burned to fumigate public gathering places—thus the word incense from incendere, to burn.

We do not know when or by whom the resins, gums, barks and woods of certain trees and shrubs were first used as fumigants, but we do know that most of them grow in the Far East, such as the frankincense and sandalwood trees, the tree from whose stems and bark camphor is derived, the tropical laurels in Asia whose inner bark is ground to make cinnamon. And we do know that the first known recipe for making a fragrant substance is set forth in Exodus 30:34, when the Lord tells Moses in explicit detail the exact proportions of necessary gums and spices to be pounded together and "put before the testimony" in the "tent of the meeting." Furthermore, He strictly forbids this precious amalgam being made by any but authorized persons.

It was natural that the use of incense as a fumigant should develop into its use as part of religious ceremonials. From the time it was used to mitigate the effluvia of slaughtered animal sacrifice up to the time when large and foul crowds gathered in the cathedrals of Europe, it gradually evolved into its symbolical use as part of religious ceremonials. The first Christians who worshiped in the catacombs burned incense as a sanitary fumigation, although it does not seem to have been incorporated into the ritual of the church until the fourth or fifth century. Thus, originally the incensing of things and persons was a purification. Then it became a symbol of consecration. Finally, a symbol of the sanctification of the soul.

Since all religions concern themselves with bodily health as well as spiritual well-being, it was inevitable that the perfume of flowers and the burning of gums and resins should find their way into the sickroom. Royalty carried bouquets to counteract the stench of medieval streets. Aromatic plants were burned to ward off plague and pestilence. When the first meeting houses were built in the new world, women carried "Sabbath posies" and "Meeting house seeds." The little bunches of southernwood, bergamot, costmary and moss roses revived their spirits against the dismal prognostications of the preacher, and the seeds of fennel and caraway which the children nibbled helped to keep them quiet.

In El Salvador there still exists in some private houses the pretty custom of a servant walking through the rooms in the early morning, waving a burning balsam branch, whose perfume seeps through the whole house.

This is Peruvian balm, which grows chiefly in El Salvador, its misnomer coming from the fact that it used originally to be shipped to Europe via Peru. Lately, trees have been planted in Ceylon and these, too, keep the familiar name. During the last world war, great quantities of it were used in first aid stations on the European battle front as an antiseptic and healing agent, and it still holds its value as a perfume base.

Thus perfume permeates the annals of mankind, and its power to cleanse the air gradually developed into its power to heal the sick, and finally merged with its power to purify the soul.

At the present moment it seems to have retrogressed, judging from various trade names and the pictures which accompany their advertising. Feminine perfumes are primarily aphrodisiacs. When a lady is well doused with some of the more violent brands a gentleman, even if his olfactories are in the blunted state referred to earlier, is supposed to be roused to behavior similar to that of animals at uninhibited seasons.

The animal products, such as ambergris, castor, civet and musk do not properly belong in a discourse on garden fragrance, although they have long been used, and continue to be, in the compounding of commercial perfumes.

Our laboratories turn out constantly improved synthetic odors, but the actual flowers which enter into the manufacture of toilet waters, lotions, colognes, lacquers, powders and all the rest, are still chiefly found in southern Europe and Asia Minor where the climate and soil are favorable to their growth. Here generations-old patience and knowledge utilize the quality and quantity of those oils which vary from season to season and vary with the age or youth of the plant. Although the cultivation of aromatic herbs for flavoring is becoming more widespread in our country, practically the only large-scale commercial extraction of the oils is in Michigan, with peppermint and spearmint, which are highly profitable in a nation of gum-chewers.

Having been thus wafted around the world from Ceylon to the catacombs, and from Moses to Michigan, we find ourselves again in our own small garden, standing, in the springtime, before a bright fraxinella, with its firm tidy leaves and its ineffable white flowers.

What a delight it is every year, from the moment it thrusts its blunt green tips above the soil until it develops into its symmetrical green form! From its flowers and foliage there rises a perfumed gas, which, on a windless summer evening, will faintly ignite if touched by a lighted match. Hence, its charming name of burning bush—or its less charming one of gas plant. It is also called dictamnus and dittany, and by any other name it would smell as sweet.

It is supposed to dislike being moved, but I have dragged mine all over the place and each time it has seemed more sturdy and shining than ever. It is sweet all day long, but in the evening its perfume intensifies, and to me this living incense which burns but does not consume itself is more affecting than any substance compounded by man. One need not grade the virtues of spring flowers, or refer to an odophone to know what perfume is pleasing. But as long as one fraxinella shines in my garden I will feel humble and grateful.

The peonies in the warming sun are like young healthy country girls who have scrubbed themselves properly and put on fresh linen for a day at the fair. They exude the wholesome odor of youth, untainted by any hint of decay or even of the fading of age. You cannot put this emanation in a bottle any more than you can fix a passing blush. Its girl-woman outdoor gaiety has nothing in common with the swooning tuberose scent of a harem odalisque or the exciting wild ginger blossom in the lei of a hula girl. A little later phlox will repeat a similar dainty and profoundly feminine perfume, without a trace of excess or finickiness.

In Virginia, honeysuckle weaves a tangled mat along roadsides and swarms over and under fences and clambers to the top of trees, so that farmers must root it up and burn it to save their pastures. But every spring it comes crowding back and infuses into the long spring evenings an ecstasy of romance that is almost anguish. When it grows in more northern latitudes it does not cover such expanses, but each honeyed blossom holds the same elixir of rapture and dreams.

In midsummer we leave the garden and tramp in the woods and along the shore where sweet fern sweeps the banks and responds to rough trampling with a breath of forgiveness. There is bay, and the aroma from the hard gray berries when rolled between the palms lasts for a long time. There is the salty smell of seaweed drying on the beach. These are wild pungencies held in memory of summer by the sea.

In early autumn friends sit in the flecked shadow of the arbor where grapes are ripening. Their scent mingles with that of the boxwood which edges the garden walks, and the ancient grapevine and ancient hedge seem a protective part of the friendship quietly exchanged.

When we cut the fall flowers the musky masculine pungence of marigold mingles with the milder tang of chrysanthemums and the sweet meek breath of petunias.

Through the cycle of the seasons emotions and fragrances proceed together. Under their enchantment it is difficult to distinguish precisely what we are smelling and what we are remembering.

But when the time comes to rake up the dried brown stalks of hollyhocks and gladioli and phlox, to pile them all and burn them—then there rises into the cool autumn sky the final incense of the gardener's year. It fulfills the original purpose of incense, for it fumigates the air and destroys any disease that may have clung to the dead rubbish. It becomes a bonfire which is a ceremonial in its own right. It smolders a long time after the glow has died down, and the smoke becomes part of the ritual which is significant according to our faith.

And lemons, citrons, dates, and oranges,
    And all the fruits whose savour is most rare,
Shall shine within the shadow of your trees;
    And every one shall be a lover there.

TRANSLATED FROM THE ITALIAN

Farewell, green fields and happy groves,
Where flocks have took delight.
Where lambs have nibbled, silent moves
The feet of angels bright;
Unseen they pour blessing,
And joy without ceasing,
On each bud and blossom,
And each sleeping bosom.

WILLIAM BLAKE

A garden is a delight to the eye, and a
solace to the soul; it soothes angry pas-
sions, and produces that pleasure which
is a foretaste of paradise.

SADI

THE SENTIMENTAL GARDEN

Bleeding-Heart
DICENTRA SPECTABILIS

Gardening is no mere pretty pastime, indulged in by ladies in shady hats and white dresses, snipping a few roses into a dainty basket. It never was.

Gardening has always been a strenuous affair, and slacks and shorts and overalls are appropriate costumes for its pursuit. Hats are optional; so are gloves. You may wear what you please as you spade up the earth, trundle the compost, water and weed. You may wear what you please, but you are not allowed to enjoy what you please, for in this day when the girl who washes your hair is a beautician and the man who sells you a coffin is a mortician, even home gardeners are professionals, or feel that they should be.

There have always been expert gardeners and there have always been landscape architects, although the term is fairly recent, and there have always been individuals whose skill and taste and knowledge have lifted them out of amateur standing. But probably never before has there been such a guilt consciousness among men and women who would otherwise be happy dabblers.

They feel guilty because they are continually being told that they don't know how to put a seed in the ground, or how to arrange a handful of tulips. They cringe because they once thought magenta petunias were pretty and that roses bloomed only in June.

They are as ashamed to have guests as the timid bride whose flat silver doesn't "match." And they are appalled by the mass of information they must assimilate before they can order half a dozen bulbs.

It seems that gardening is not primarily a diversion but a business, and a grim one at that.

This is not to imply that anyone without experience or the rudiments of knowledge can rush forth, plant a garden in a few hours and have specimen blooms—or any blooms—from May until frost. We all have to learn, but the learning should be as much of a pleasure as putting it into practice. We should be willing for our growing wisdom to unfold as the flowers themselves unfold, so that our saunter down the garden path is a happy diversion instead of a groaning pilgrim's progress.

Public opinion is heavily weighted against the sentimental gardener. This is the obstinate creature who is too tender-hearted to cut down a tree or even prune a branch to open a vista; who is too stingy to dig out and throw away—or even give away—perennials that are too crowded or unsatisfactory in form or color. Age, which is supposed to harden the heart as well as the arteries, makes him more mushy, and discrimination, which should come with experience, is not in his lexicon. And so he pushes his way through a tangle of growing things that grow into barriers, muffle outlines and shut off the breeze.

Like many weak creatures, this sentimentalist has extraordinary tenacity. He keeps his clutter because he loves it, and because every spear and leaf has some association which is dearer than the over-all effect.

This wild columbine, with leaves too small and blossoms too meager, was brought from the woods one enchanted April day and the memories it touches are more precious than pride in the newest long-spurred hybrid. The first clump of this *Phlox divaricata,* which is now a mat encroaching on the primroses, was given him long ago by a friend for his first funny little border. There are improved varieties, with blossoms bigger and bluer, but these particular ones remind him of the friend he loved and the blossoms which look mediocre to everyone else are big enough and blue enough for him. Well he knows that a clump of gaillardia would give a vigorous accent to that scraggly corner, but he doesn't like gaillardias. Well he knows that nasturtiums are common things, but these gypsy dancers give him delight and he intends to have them—old-fashioned single ones—masses of them, to run like fires which brighten but do not scorch the edge of his border.

So he plants and preserves what he likes, and is happily unconcerned by supercilious glances of visitors who follow precepts instead of emotions.

The sentimental gardener takes his first step on the downward path when he draws up the list of the guests he will invite to his garden party. Not for him to ask the service of an Elsa Maxwell to select those who should be asked, and to determine their proper placing. No, indeed, he will ask whom he pleases, and if they don't get along together that is a minor matter.

Since even the sentimental gardener has learned from previous years some of the mistakes inherent in such a policy, he determines to do a little better this year.

I remember the time I invited the Mexican four-o'clocks and they came rushing in fluttering full skirts and appropriated the whole place so boisterously I had to shoo them out. Half a dozen times I have coaxed the antirrhinum to attend and although it grudgingly made an appearance, it has been a sulky one. The dianthus has a way of getting bedraggled before the party is half over. In spite of the salvia having been to finishing school, she is apt to revert to her original shrewish ways and quarrel with everything else. The bachelor's buttons and larkspur lose their natty spruceness and wander seedily all over the place. Away with them until they have learned how to behave or, perhaps, until we have learned how to handle them. And that new rose, whose portrait and description in the catalogue promised so much! She arrived on time, gave one brief ineffable smile, and then for the rest of the evening merely took up too much room, demanded too much food and never twinkled another blushing smile. Even the gladioli, like gawky English girls with exquisite complexions, who have been brought from the schoolroom to the drawing-room before they have learned how to carry themselves—they must develop a better posture before they are asked.

Of course, there are the familiar and faithful perennials who will come as a matter of course, just as certain relatives and old friends must always attend every celebration. We don't omit Aunt Clara because she has grown so fat, or Uncle Bob because he has become a bit tedious, and it would take a harder heart than most of us possess to root out a huge and healthy bleeding-heart because its corolla is not precisely the right shade, or discard a sturdy phlox because its conversation—in this case its florets—is not as satisfactory as it might be. We shall keep the old standbys—that is, most of them—even if they are not quite up to the mark. We forgive them their faults of niggardliness or superabundance, but it is hard to be amiable when they commit the social error of staying too long.

Chrysanthemums, for instance. How delightful to welcome them when most of the other guests are going or have gone. Fresh and fine and lavishly attired, they come stamping in and fill up the thinning room with their vigorous personalities. Splendid! We *are* glad to see them. But, gradually, as the house empties and the dining room, which looked so festive with its joyous throng, takes on a disordered appearance with empty spaces on the once care-fully arranged tables, the hostess grows a bit fatigued. She would like to clean up the whole mess and go to bed, for it has been a long hullabaloo from start to finish.

But you can't begin chucking stained linen into cold water and picking up broken glasses and emptying ashtrays so long as there are still merrymakers waving their hands and bobbing their heads and calling to one another. You can't do a thorough job of pulling up the dead annuals and getting in fertilizer and compost and transplanting spring perennials so long as the garden is more or less filled with chrysanthemums. Of course, you can cut down all the blooms and chop down the stalks, but even if your vases, and your neighbors' vases, would hold them all, it is unthinkable to denude a still sparkling garden any more than to turn out revelers who don't know enough to go home.

Long after midnight the petunias are sprawling and clamber-ing and budding all over the place, their faces as fresh and their leaves as green as if they had just arrived. It is not their fault. I sent them seed invitations with a lavish hand and they have man-fully borne the brunt and heat of the long summer and done their best—and a very good best—to make the garden party a success. But until they clear out I can't repair the gap which in April be-longs to the *Saxatile compacta*. By the time these lingering guests have taken themselves off it may be too late to prepare for an early spring breakfast.

I have been through all this many times, and each year I re-solve that I will plan my next garden party with firmness and commonsense. I won't have a carousing omnium gatherum. I'll have a select and dignified reception, and I will not be imposed upon by hangers-on. And even as I make this resolution I know that sentimentality will seep in and swamp me. The reason is obvious. My head is ruled by my heart and I need no psycho-analysis to tell me I prefer it so.

For to me a garden is not so much a picture to be painted as a place to find pleasure, and its impression on others is not as important as its satisfaction to me.

So I will make no further resolutions to be a person of firm caliber, but will maunder around in my own way. There are many departments of life in which we must conform to regimented standards. The garden is not one of them. I have no sense of obligation but only anticipation of personal pleasure. If I learn a little every year—and it is impossible to avoid a modicum of accumulated knowledge—that will be another pleasure, but I will learn it the easy way, which is the way of the sentimentalist.

I will keep my wild columbine because of one day in April and the *Phlox divaricata* because every spring it speaks to me of my friend who gave it to me many years ago.

I have neither space nor skill to maintain a rose garden, and were I to start on such a venture I would be utterly bewildered before I had read one page of one catalogue. There are teas and hybrids; there are bedding, shrub, tree, hedge and climbing roses. There are everblooming and perpetual and polyantha roses. Every year new ones are introduced—prize winners, patented and those named for illustrious people.

In this glorious and multitudinous assortment I do not find a certain Killarney rose. Occasionally there is an inconspicuous listing of a double white Killarney, and I am sure it is charming, but the one I mean is pink, with a slenderly pointed bud opening into a sweet and modest flower. Although I do not happen to find it in the catalogues I could doubtless get it from some nursery.

But I do not need to purchase it for I already possess it.

It is not so grand as many of its sisters. Indeed, it is hardly noticed by anyone but me. But I expect to keep it as long as I have a garden on this earth, and I will never be able to look at it without a deep warmth in my heart. For this is the rose above all others that my mother especially loved.

" 'Tis well said," said Candide, "and now we must cultivate our garden."

VOLTAIRE

Poppy

PAPAVER ORIENTALE

When the first green spears appear in the garden in the spring-time, they are accompanied by a similar phenomenon in the heart of the gardener, like Swedenborg's doctrine of correspondences. According to that metaphysician, there are two worlds: one of nature and one of the spirit. These are distinct but intimately connected. Each has its atmosphere, its own waters and earth, and the causes of all things in the spiritual world are the effects of all things in the natural world, like the concave and convex surfaces of the same object.

These manifestations, when applied to gardens, are discon-certing. For while we like to think that the floral habits of the natural world are beautiful and orderly and good, we observe with dismay that their correspondences in the spiritual world are very bad indeed.

The deplorable situation begins with inconspicuous trifles.

Impatience to see the first true leaves of the pansies pushes aside what should be a surge of joyous anticipation. Procrastination follows impatience. Not procrastination in regard to the garden, for even the novice soon appreciates that seasons and weather wait for no man, but in regard to practically every other rational obligation. We are so busy transplanting the snapdragons, we cannot spare time to call on a bereaved or convalescing friend. We keep luncheon and dinner waiting for just a few moments—for half an hour —to the inconvenience or exasperation of the cook, while we finish marking off the space for the zinnia seeds. The excited gardener, digging, weeding, pruning, fertilizing, ignores normal consideration for household, family and friends. He is obsessed by his passion, and as the season progresses his moral fiber progressively deteriorates. Amenities, like respect for appearances, vanish soon on the swift journey. We design our gardens to make a pleasing picture and we ourselves, in dirt-stained clothes and grubby paws, are moving scarecrows amid the pristine verdure. The male or female form, bent double in absorbed labor, is—especially from the rear, where it is most often observed—a slightly comic and wholly unattractive sight. But who, planting a Chinese bellflower, remembers that in the garden of Yang Kuei-fei it was commanded that peonies must be tended only by maidens in rich attire, while winter pears should be nurtured by wan, esthetic priests? Who, attacking compost, loam and sand, clad in overalls, slacks or shorts, remembers Byrsa in Carthage, where the lovely hill on which stands the convent of Les Pères Blancs, is made more lovely by the moving figures of the white-robed monks? Perhaps we have seen this, perhaps we have only seen pictures of it, but in either case it is obliterated from our thoughts as we plunge into our sweaty jobs and wipe our soil-stained brows with grimy hands.

These are small matters compared to what is to come, and are mentioned merely to show the insidious infiltration of larger, and ultimately major, vices.

Hypocrisy follows. We exclaim with false flattery when our neighbor's daffodils are sweeping the hillside, while ours are still obstinate tight buds. Disloyalty presses at the heels of hypocrisy, for we look with shame at an unsymmetrical shrub, as a heartless parent might avert eyes from a child unfortunate enough to have a harelip.

Membership in a garden club is more dangerous than signing up with the Communist party. Such organizations seem cunningly designed to lure us away from enjoying a garden for itself. It accomplishes its final purpose when our own garden ceases to be a haven of repose and is valued primarily as a social gesture, to be exhibited on the proper day and at the proper hour to other garden club members, in the malicious hope that it will humble them from happy human beings into miserable inferiority complexes.

We go from bad to worse. Stinginess in parting with some choice bulb or root is only one step from covetousness, which is only one step away from stealing. Stealing is a legal crime, a moral vice and a religious sin, but otherwise honorable men and women, succumbing to the temptation of possessing a flower that does not belong to them, have become, without a qualm, common thieves.

The roster is long and shameful. / to p. 107

The crocus was first brought to England by a pilgrim who had seen it in Persia, where its theft was a crime punishable by death. This man of God made a hollow in his sacred staff and smuggled a purloined bulb in it. He managed to get it to Saffron Waldron in Cambridgeshire, where it brought forth the first crocus in Britain. For this he considered himself, and has been subsequently considered, a benefactor to his country.

Secular as well as religious dignitaries have brazenly joined the ranks of pilferers. A worthy and industrious florist in Paris imported at great expense a rare variety of anemone. He guarded it for ten harassed years, until the time should come when he could establish his fame and fortune. A highly placed French councillor begged, or possibly commanded, the privilege of viewing the treasured bed when the plants were in seed. With apparent carelessness he dropped his woolen cloak on one and his servant, who had been instructed and rehearsed, picked it up promptly and folded it in such a way that some of the seeds stuck to the rough material, and that was the end of the florist's monopoly.

Royal persons have been both the victims and perpetrators of such embezzlements.

The Empress Josephine, who was an idolater of flowers, had never seen a dahlia until she left her birthplace of Martinique and went to France. The Swedish botanist Dahl had brought this plant to such perfection that it was named for him, and he honored the sovereign by giving her some bulbs which she planted with her own hands at Malmaison. At the proper season it was her custom to invite princes and ministers to view her treasures, but she would never allow a seed or a blossom to go out of her possession. A Polish prince did not consider it a betrayal of hospitality to bribe a gardener to filch some seeds, nor did he consider it extravagant to tempt the poor fellow with a louis apiece for them. They bloomed for him as they bloom for us, and the Empress was so consumed with jealousy that she would never again have another dahlia.

The Jardim Botanico in Rio de Janeiro is a vast and topless temple, with three radiating aisles, their six thousand feet bordered by precisely planted palms, as impressive as the rearing columns of Karnak. The trunks are gray, their monotone softened by green and rosy moss and by infinitesimal clinging ferns. There are specimens from many parts of the world: date palms from Africa, coconut palms from Polynesia, the palm from which fiber hats are made and one from whose seeds buttons are made, each one inconspicuously but clearly labeled with its name, number and place of its origin.

Apart from the rest stands the mother of all the royal palms in Brazil. She rises from a little altar, with a stone tablet at her feet to tell that she was planted in 1808 by Dom João VI, whose bronze bust is placed facing her. Dom João had a fancy to keep this imported tree unique, and he ordered every seed which fell to be burned. Like the English dovecot which was once permitted only to the nobility and the clergy, the palm was to be exclusive to royalty. But slaves—who unfortunately had the same low morals as the English monk, the French councillor and the Polish prince—stole the seeds and sold them, so that today the feather duster of the gods waves from every hillside and terrace. It may be added that the seeds are distributed free from the Botanical Garden to whoever wants them.

Once the prolific old mother was sick and there was great anxiety lest she die, but medicinal baths and treatments restored her, and when last I saw her, her once-smooth trunk was a bit whiskery and hoary but her crown of verdure, a hundred and fifteen feet above my head, was still green and vigorous. The bronze bust of Dom João seems rather insignificant compared to this doughty dowager who has lived to count her progeny by thousands.

The affinity between flowers and pilfering is acknowledged in Hungary where verbena is called the lock-opening herb. A professional thief makes a small cut in the palm of his hand and inserts a sliver of leaf into it. When the wound grows over, such a hand can open all bolts and bars at a touch. The mistletoe has been credited with similar power.

Robberies are bad enough, but wars are worse, and here again flowers are too often the *casus belli*.

Omitting the Wars of the Roses, to which flowers merely lent their names, we might begin with the "cold war" in Holland in the seventeenth century. The sudden mania for tulips precipitated a wild competition in which speculators lost their heads and their fortunes simultaneously. It was not unusual for a single bulb to fetch thousands of florins. Sometimes the actual bulb did not change hands, but merely served as a gambling symbol. In other instances, the bulb did not exist at all. There were genuine sales as well as spurious ones. A "Semper Augustus" is recorded to have been bought for thirteen thousand florins. Cornelius van Baerle's La Tulipe Noire won a prize of a hundred thousand florins. The frantic buying, selling, speculating and swindling so shook the country financially that at last the Government interfered and put down such gambling, and the price of "Semper Augustus" fell to fifty florins.

Battles precipitated by flowers have not been confined to such bloodless if sordid operations. One of the most shameful wars in all history centers around the innocent-looking poppy—*Papaver somniferum*. This modest plant was introduced into China by the Arabs, probably in the thirteenth century, and its use was chiefly medicinal. It was not until the seventeenth century that the Chinese began to smoke it as a narcotic. Its fearful effect upon the hundreds of thousands who became addicts was recognized by the government and by the imperial authorities, who forbade its importation and raised the penalty for opium smoking to banishment and even death. The long struggle culminated in the opium wars which were forced upon China by the British, who were determined to continue their traffic in the drug. The British succeeded, and by the Treaty of Nanking in 1842 the importation of opium was legalized in 1858—with results too well known and too painful to need recital here.

The fleur-de-lis was forbidden during the French Revolution and hundreds who were found wearing it were condemned to death, and the mob took furious glee in destroying those sculptures and architectural motifs in which it appeared.

The breadfruit, with its immense and decorative leaves and its mild nutritious fruit, might seem to epitomize peaceful living, since it springs up profusely in tropical climates and its satisfying and delicious food may be had for the gathering. Yet it was around this blameless tree that there swirled, in 1787, the wild and bloody massacre which has been recorded in *Mutiny on the Bounty*.

At that time the breadfruit did not grow in the West Indies and some of the British merchants and planters there, thinking it would be a cheap and wholesome food for their Negro slaves, petitioned the Crown for a vessel to be fitted out to bring back some trees from Tahiti and Owyhee. It was the *Bounty* under Captain Bligh which made the long trip to the East Indies and it was David Nelson, the botanist, who supervised the selection, purchase and lifting of the trees from their habitat to the ship.

The breadfruit, like the banana, is propagated not by seeds but by new shoots which spring up from the old roots. Nelson, as will be remembered by those who read the book or saw the moving picture based upon it, had potted the strong young handsome trees, gathering them and caring for them with infinite pains. "To obtain them men had suffered hardships, braved unknown seas and sailed more than twenty-seven thousand miles in fair weather and foul." After the mutiny "a line of men formed on the ladderway and passed the pots from hand to hand. A man by the rail aft, pulled up each young plant by the roots and flung it overboard, while others emptied the earth into the sea." More than a thousand young breadfruit trees, all in flourishing condition, were thus jettisoned, and as the *Bounty* moved away, "the wake of their rich green foliage was left tossing on the blue swell."

And what shall be said of a crime which shocked the world within the last decade, concerning Vaviloff? This handsome giant of a man, who was the head of the "Department of Agriculture" in Russia, was a plant breeder and a geneticist, leading expeditions to South America, Asia and Africa, and bringing back with him thousands of plants to enrich his native land. Never before have such vast importations been recorded, and never before were such energy and scientific research joined in glorious endeavor and achievement.

Vaviloff's reputation extended far beyond Russia, for he was elected an honorary member of the Botanical Society of America which recognizes only those who have distinguished themselves in the field of research.

It may be recalled that at this time Russia had just discovered the Darwinian theory and had excitedly adopted the belief that environment and not heredity is the controlling factor in evolution. Vaviloff's work did not fit into this ideology. It was not foreign plants which should be imported or native plants which should be altered. Environmental conditions only should be altered to promote agriculture. The matter was not allowed to remain in the realm of verbal controversy. Vaviloff's ideology conflicted with the newly embraced national idea. Therefore, the greatest scientific ambassador Russia had ever had disappeared in that prompt and undefined fashion characteristic of the Politburo.

The magnificent work he had started was handed over to Lysenko, a follower of Michurin, who is the Burbank of Russia. Lysenko is a Darwinian environmentalist and at last reports was still alive.

Among the crimes associated with plants this surely holds eminence.

The long history of robbery, deception and murder in which flowers are the incentive and the reward rises in a crashing crescendo under the spur of still another vice—prodigality.

Every devoted gardener yields at times—times more and more frequent in his career—to investing a disproportionate amount of his income in his garden, although, oddly enough, this is usually indulgently regarded as a virtue. If Mr. Jones goes without tobacco and whisky to buy a precious bulb, it might, indeed, be laudable. But if he withholds cash which Mrs. Jones sorely needs for sheets or a new stove, and spends it for a rare shrub, this is also marked down to his credit.

These are small and private matters, but, carried to excess, they have resulted in national catastrophes. Chinese dynasties have been bankrupted and overthrown through extravagant expenditure on royal pleasure gardens.

As long ago as 1766 B.C. a ruler of Hsiea filled a pool with rice wine, over which he carried his guests in barges. At the stroke of a gong, they leaped overboard and drank—and his outraged subjects deposed him.

Another emperor, Yu, squandered his entire substance on gardens for his favorite concubine, Paossu. This regal tribute must have been quite wasted, for Paossu was so capricious that she refused to be pleased by the rustle of wind in the leaves or the murmur of running water, but would vouchsafe a smile only when she listened to the sound of silk being torn. These colossal absurdities came to an abrupt end when Paossu was murdered, the garden obliterated and the line of Chou extinguished.

If these legends are a bit misty, there are sad and incontrovertible facts and figures leading to the overthrow of the Manchu Dynasty in 1911. Revenues had been set aside to build up the Chinese navy, and the Empress Dowager calmly appropriated them to make her summer palace and build up its gardens. When war with Japan was declared, China found herself with only a marble boat moored to the shore and a few barges, and the Dragon Throne was lost.

Such scattered facts are merely a few in the indictment against gardens, which includes breaking practically all of the Ten Commandments. What gardener worthy of the name observes the Sabbath day as specified in the Decalogue? What gardener has not cursed aloud at the advent of slugs, scale, leaf-miners and beetles? Killing one's enemies—or one's friends—to get possession of a plant may be a bit out of date, but stealing, bearing false witness and coveting our neighbor's goods are current commonplaces. The seventh commandment—if we make a survey of literature from the *Decameron* to the latest issue of popular magazines—is fre quently and enthusiastically broken in a garden.

Obviously, the intemperate love of gardening—and wha profound love is ever temperate?—begins with personal pecca dillos and leads to national disasters and moral disintegration.

What, then, can a garden offer to offset these crimes?

What defense can the gardener plead?

Humbly he can offer a few virtues which have grown from the same soil as the many vices.

He can offer faith, for every seed that is sown is a testament of belief in a living future.

He can offer hope, which is foster-sister to faith, and sustains him through the coldest spring, the hottest summer, the most drenching autumn and the most savage winter.

And, finally, he can offer—in fact, he cannot withhold— love.

Love, which is variously defined in dictionaries, needs no definition by those who have experienced it. We know it quite well when, in the springtime, we gaze at the star-shaped flowers of *Ornithogalum,* the petals incandescently white, the beadlike center glisteningly black. We know it quite well when we are lost in ecstasy before a peerless Madonna lily. We know it when our hearts are lifted and sustained, after all the other flowers are gone, and the brave and brilliant chrysanthemums gush forth in final triumphant glory.

We experience the purest love not only for individual flowers, but love and gratitude to the whole plan of creation which brings forth such miracles. Faith in this plan and its Creator, and hope that we may share, in still another year, its blessing and its grace.

Faith, hope and love. We are assured on the best authority that these are the supreme virtues.

Perhaps they will serve to counterbalance the vices engendered by a garden.

Sweet Breeze.

Sweet breeze that sett'st the summer buds a-swaying,
Dear lambs amid the primrose meadows playing,
Let me not think!
O floods, upon whose brink
The merry birds are maying,
Dream, softly dream! O blessed mother, lead me
Unsevered from thy girdle—lead me! feed me!
I have no will but thine;
I need not but the juice
Of elemental wine—
Perish remoter use
Of strength reserved for conflict yet to come!
Let me be dumb!
As long as I may feel thy hand—
This, this is all—do ye not understand
How the great Mother mixes all our bloods?
O breeze! O swaying buds!
O lambs, O primroses, O floods!

T. E. BROWN

From *Collected Poems of T. E. Brown.* By permission of The Macmillan Company, publishers.

NO SPEECH NOR LANGUAGE

Primrose

PRIMULA INTERMEDIA

In a world where nations are separated by many different languages and where there are too many written and spoken words in all of them, it might seem that there would be a sufficient number to meet all exigencies.

Human beings have been talking for a long time. The Book of Genesis states that originally "the whole earth was of one language and of one speech," which admirable arrangement was broken up by no less than the Lord Himself. For, in punishment of a people who were so presumptuous that they planned to build a tower whose top should reach to heaven, He confounded their language so that they could not understand one another and scattered them abroad upon the face of the earth.

The destruction of the tower of Babel did not discourage the human race. It has gone on talking, with ever-increasing vocabularies and ever-increasing methods of transmission, translation and intercommunication, paralleled by sciences of philology and phonetics which, like the ill-fated tower of Babel, reach toward heaven

And, in spite of it all, there are occasions and ceremonies when there are no words to express our intentions or emotions, and we have to turn to flowers and leaves and trees which have never made the slightest effort toward vocality.

We depend upon their statements or intercessions in the only three events in our individual lives which are considered worthy of statistical and genealogical record—birth, marriage and death.

At the birth of a son or daughter, we do occasionally plant a tree, and even the least sentimental among us hestitates before cutting down one which commemorates some ancestor. Certain primitive tribes believe the life of a newborn child is bound with the life of the tree planted on the day of its birth. In some parts of Switzerland an apple tree is planted for a boy and a pear tree for a girl, and there are families in Russia, France, Germany, Italy and England which follow the ancient custom. But nowadays in these countries it is more of a pretty gesture than a formal rite. Trees are no longer necessary and visible registers as they were, for instance, in the Malay Archipelago. Here it was customary to plant a clove tree at the birth of each child, and when the Dutch government ordered twenty-five thousand of these cut down, the edict precipitated a native insurrection. In the light of our own program of price control of agricultural products, it is easy to understand why the Dutch wanted to restrict the valuable crop. But we may not understand that the natives rose in fury not because of an economic measure forced upon them, but because the cloves were birth trees, as valuable to them as our legally inscribed and preserved registries.

If we no longer call for the testimony of trees, plants and flowers to assist in the celebration of a birth, we still invite a whole cloud of floral witnesses or their representatives to every wedding. Such witnesses are the orange blossoms on the veil or on the prayer book of our most modern bride. These fragile flowers draw

fter them whole centuries of nuptial association. The ancient Sara-
ens believed them an augury of fecundity, since in the East the
range tree may be seen blossoming and bearing fruit at the same
me. Therefore, the little Saracen brides wore them woven into
arlands for their heads, and the Crusaders brought the fashion, if
ot the belief, back with them to England. In Crete both bride
nd bridegroom were perfumed with orange water, and in Sardinia
ranges were fastened to the horns of the oxen which drew the
edding carriage.

With us, today, the more durable bouvardia and stephanotis
nd tuberose often serve as substitutes for the delicate orange blos-
om, and it must be admitted that guests at a fashionable wedding
nay view the whole business of flowers with cynicism. For their
whiteness politely, if not accurately, indicates purity, their quantity
ndicates expense, and the carefully carried prayer book, with its
ribbons and bouquet, is merely a decorative adjunct. However, it
s not impossible that these things were true in Arabia, and that
similar disrespectful observations might have been made at Cretan
and Sardinian weddings.

The inconspicuous rosemary was, for hundreds of years, almost as eloquent an attendant at weddings as the orange blossom.
It was entwined in the bridal wreath as a symbol of remembrance,
so that the wife should carry with her to her new home loving
memories of her old. It also signified fidelity, and Anne of Cleves,
who wore it to her marriage with Henry VIII, may later have
pondered this.

Its mute but ubiquitous presence at weddings was not all
that was expected of the rosemary. It was equally in demand at
funerals, although at the former the sprigs were dipped in scented
water and for the latter plain water was sufficient. The mourners,
walking or being carried through the medieval streets, held bits of
rosemary in their hands and dropped them upon the coffin after
it had been lowered into the ground, and later rosemary was often

planted upon graves. Often a spray was placed in the hands of the dead, just as in small German villages it was customary to place acorns in such hands, or to put an apple in the palm of a dead child, so he would have something to play with in Paradise.

We do not plant rosemary in our gardens as often as we used to do, but we cannot banish it from our literature, where its name is a synonym for memory.

If the three solemnest events—birth, marriage and death—have called on plants, seeds, leaves and flowers as participants, so do lesser observances.

Honor and fame are so universally expressed by wreaths of laurel that the words are almost interchangeable. The poet laureate of England carries the syllables in his title, as do those thousands of sermons preached every commencement time when bachelors receive their degrees of baccalaureates.

As some flowers serve as substitutes for the spoken word, or as shorthand symbols for the written one, so others are the stock in trade of cartoonists, becoming actual ideographs. Ever since the dove brought the olive leaf to Noah, the olive has signified peace. Ever since the ancient Romans gave a palm to the victors of games, the palm has signified success.

Heraldry, which is a tiny facet of history, draws heavily upon floral emblems to summarize significant events.

The fleur-de-lis is a striking example of this. When Louis VII of France (1137–1180) was excommunicated by the Pope, he decided to join the Crusaders, and for his blazon he chose the fleur-de-lis. (Incidentally, this flower so often referred to as a lily is no lily at all, but our familiar purple iris.) Whether Louis called it the fleur-de-Louis in honor of himself—from which it was corrupted into fleur-de-luce and then into fleur-de-lis—or whether it commemorates the last syllable of Clovis, which is the same as lovis or louis, is debatable. At any event, Louis VII had his flag thickly sewn with lilies as he set forth on his pilgrimage. Charles VI, who

cceeded him, reduced the number to three in honor of the Holy
rinity.

This insigne of the three lilies was so proudly held by the
rench that when Edward III of England wanted to record that
e had claimed the nominal dignity of the French sovereign, he
ad the fleur-de-lis taken away from the armorial bearings of the
tter. As the balance of power shifted back and forth, so did the
orm and position of the lilies. Edward, to denote his maternal de-
cent from Isabel, the daughter and heiress of Philip IV of France,
uartered his arms with those of France. Fourteen years later, when
e claimed that kingdom, he placed the lilies in the first quarter,
efore the arms of England.

Edward had used only the seeds of the lily, but when Henry
V claimed the sovereignty of France, not nominally but actually,
e quartered not the seeds but the full fleur-de-lis as the French
ings had done. He also replaced the English arms in the first
uarter as the position of greatest honor.

The switching back and forth continued. When, in Paris,
Henry VI was crowned King of France, he had the fleur-de-lis
gain placed in the first quarter of the English escutcheon. It was
till there when George I ascended the throne in 1714 and there
: remained until the reign of George III. Then, in 1800, when
reland was joined to England, some modification of the national
nsignia was in order. The King of England dropped the title of
King of France, and the fleur-de-lis was removed from the royal
rms. Although Napoleon put the bee in place of the lily, this
nnovation was temporary. The fleur-de-lis is still the badge of
France.

Thus, those who can decipher heraldic emblems can, by
ollowing the placing and form of the fleur-de-lis, read seven cen-
uries of French and English history.

Flowers have long done duty as silent slogans for nationalistic
or patriotic bodies. Just as the red rose was the crest of the House

of Lancaster and the white rose of the House of York, so was the red lily the badge of the Guelphs and the white the badge of the Ghibellines. It is as impossible to imagine Scotland without the thistle as Ireland without the shamrock. When Geoffrey of Anjou was going to battle, he plucked a golden spray of the broom plant —*Genista*—which was growing on the heath and fastened it in his helmet. "Planta genista!" his soldiers cried, as they followed the bright signal. It waved triumphantly throughout the fray and thereupon became his badge and that of his descendants, being embroidered upon their dress and worked into their jewelry. Oddly enough, the wild shrub which is called broom in most places throughout the United States is still called plantagenet in certain parts of Cape Cod, where it blooms on the low rolling moors.

If these events seem far away, there are familiar festivals in our busy and practical lives which would not be complete without the verdant plant whose symbolism is rooted in myth.

For most Christian merrymakers the mistletoe is the one with the most ancient lineage of them all, and for those who are interested in such things it utters whole volumes of folklore, custom and superstitions.

It is first heard of when Baldur, son of Odin, was slain with a spear made from the mistletoe, which was the only thing in the created world which had not sworn never to harm this wisest, mildest and most beautiful of the immortals.

It emerges from Scandinavian myth to become part of the ceremonial rites of the Druids, for whom the mistletoe and the oak on which it grew were sacred—so sacred, indeed, that the very name of the Druids is believed to mean merely "oak men." Pliny described in detail how the Druids cut the mistletoe on the sixth day of the moon, which dated the beginning of their months, of their years and of their thirty years' cycle. He tells how, after preparation for the sacrifice and feast had been made under the oak tree, two white bulls whose horns had never before been ound, were brought to the tree. A priest clad in white climbed up and with a golden sickle cut the mistletoe, which was caught in a white cloth. Only then could the sacrifice and feast proceed. The Druids believed that whatever grew on an oak was sent from heaven and, therefore, the mystical spray was cut not with a common knife but with a sickle of gold and not permitted to touch the earth when it fell.

The worship of the mistletoe and the belief in its healing power spread all over the world, and the peculiar respect inspired by it seems never to have wholly died. Thus, the Italian peasant still believes the mistletoe extinguishes fire. In Bohemia it is hung up to prevent houses being struck by lightning, and in Wales it used to be given to the first cow to calve after the first hour of the New Year, to give luck to the dairy.

These facts, fancies and fictions, and a hundred more, are in the voice of the mistletoe, not less eloquent for being unheard by those hurrying thousands who, at Christmas time, buy a spray of the traditional green with its white berries, tie it with white ribbon and use it as decoration and a sanction—no longer needed —for kisses.

The instinct to associate flowers with human traits and ideas, while universal, is worked out in great detail by the Chinese. Thus, with them, the pomegranate, with its many seeds, indicates fertility; the fungus, longevity; the cedar, enduring virtue; the mulberry leaf, successful endeavor. The umbrella tree should be planted near libraries, since the phoenix, bringer of inspiration, was supposed to light on it, and so on through a long list of categories.

The symbolism of many flowers is by no means intricate. Pansies, with their bland or puzzled faces, are unmistakably for thoughts—*pensées*. Someone would certainly have put the lucky clover on playing cards today if it had not been done centuries ago.

The sunflower, turning throughout the day toward the sun, is for constancy, and poets and artists have loved it dearly. Whoever has visited the church of St. Remi at Rheims, remembers the twelfth-century stained glass window in the apse. The Virgin and St. John stand on either side of the Cross, their heads encircled by aureoles whose outer circles are sunflowers. These are turned toward the Saviour, as toward their true sun.

Such symbols are by no means confined to the past.

Flowers tenaciously hold their place in our most elaborate public ceremonies and in our simplest private actions. They enter into the making of laws, as when solid men with determined faces gather to debate, earnestly and even hotly, which flower should be nominated and voted upon to represent their particular one of the United States, although there should be nothing difficult about such a decision, since the native flower which blooms most profusely is the obvious choice.

Industries are built upon flowers, as armies and phalanxes of florists apply themselves to the making of funeral sprays and wreaths, automatically following the conventional rules: white flowers and white streamers for a child; purple flowers and white ribbons for adults; purple flowers and black streamers for the aged.

Communication and transportation systems concern themselves with the matter, as telegraph offices click out messages for flowers ordered in Minnesota to be delivered in Massachusetts, and airplanes make special provision to carry blossoms which opened in Hawaii on one day to be worn in Oregon the next.

Social observances consider them, for Emily Post says explicitly that no more than three gardenias should be worn at one time, and tells how bouquets and corsages should be presented to speakers and guests of honor at luncheons and dinners.

Before the telegraph and the airplane, people sent flowers to friends who were ill, to express affection, and to friends who had died, to express grief. What words were there then, or are there now, to convey these emotions? Long after the kindly arbiter of etiquette has gone hence, lovers will carry flowers to their sweethearts, and sometimes the gardenias will be more than three, and sometimes the offering will be simple posies from their mothers' gardens or even from the meadows. Lovers have never been lacking in loquacity, but even they find they cannot say all that is in their hearts and that flowers—and only flowers—can say it for them.

It is obvious why flowers should be part of every hour and season and occasion in a country like Hawaii. No matter how many leis are made of the fresh ginger and jasmine, carnations and gardenias; no matter if these fragrant wreaths are piled six and eight deep over the shoulders of every arriving and departing visitor, there are always more to be had for the picking. Hibiscus blooms are sometimes affixed to long, pencil-thin stalks of bamboo, which are spread, fanlike, in a vase. Each blossom lives only for a day, but the next day there are more to replace the faded ones.

It is more remarkable when flowers are conspicuous in countries where their growing entails much labor and expense. In Iceland, for instance, there are miles and miles of greenhouses in those sections where they can be heated with water from the natural hot springs. Although such heat is plentiful and not prohibitive in price, the pipes, the glass, even the wood and bricks and cement used in the construction of the houses must be imported, so that the finished building represents a heavy expenditure. And in these precious enclosures at least half the space, and sometimes all of it, is given over not to vegetables and fruits, but to flowers. There are some tomatoes and cucumbers, to be sure. It is possible to raise grapes and even bananas. But these are regarded as luxuries, while flowers are a necessity. The greengrocer may have nothing green to offer, but the florists' windows are brilliant. Even when flowers are growing abundantly out-of-doors during the summer, the florist's business is assured. For no christening or wedding, no funeral or celebration, formal or casual, can proceed without flowers. A conservatory opening out of a room in a private house is a miracle of succeeding bloom and tended with love and labor through the twelve months of the year.

If the amount of space and money devoted to flowers in Iceland seems almost disproportionate, another northern people have made a highly practical compromise.

The Swedes, who have a remarkable faculty for balancing sense and sentiment, had an excellent idea when they founded in Stockholm the Flower Foundation. Alma Hedin, sister of the explorer, started the idea of people sending some of the money they would otherwise spend on flowers for funerals to a fund which would, in time, provide a model home at very low rent for aged people. The gift of money should be sent to the office of the Flower Fund, which in turn sends a card to the family of the deceased, explaining the use to which the money is being put and expressing the sender's sympathy.

The idea was introduced in 1918 and by 1924 the Fund was able to erect its first building on a site donated by the city, and before the old people could move in, the foundation for a larger building was laid beside it. These houses contain small apartments —planned and decorated with the practicality and exquisite taste for which the Swedes are noted. During the ten years following the first house, six additional ones were built, each of them with a laundry and a bakery, beside the restaurants which serve meals in the dining rooms or send them to the lodgers' rooms if they do not want to use their individual kitchens. There is nothing institutional about these homes. Lodgers pay a much lower rent and receive more comfortable and attractive quarters than they could get elsewhere, and are entitled to a certain amount of attention from the resident nurse. For the rest, they are entirely independent, and the spacious, well-kept gardens around each home are for their use and pleasure.

Today there are about a hundred Flower Fund Associations in various cities in Sweden, and several have been modeled after them in Greater New York.

There persists, however, in the human heart an instinct to send to those friends whose visible forms are now sealed away in dateless night, a token whose freshness will hardly outlive the day. The paradox is deeper than reason, as love is deeper than thought. The florists in Stockholm were not enthusiastic when the Flower Fund first started. But while it is generously and steadily supported by contributions which would otherwise have been spent on wreaths and sprays, the florists need not have worried. People still send flowers in Sweden.

The day when all the people of the world were one, and had one language, ended abruptly with the destruction of the tower of Babel. Since then men have been busily splitting up into groups whose distrust of one another is intensified by their inability to talk together.

In modern times, the Finns have synthesized a language which is unintelligible to other Scandinavians. The Irish have insisted upon reintroducing Gaelic, to the confusion not only of the English but of themselves. Even the remote Faroese have followed a similar venture. There are about twenty-five thousand of these hardy folk, and they subsist upon a handful of bleak islands which are separated from the rest of the world and, during the long winter, from one another. One might think these few isolated families would shun any step that would put them farther apart from outer civilization. But not at all. They have revived their ancient spoken tongue, and even formulated a Faroese-Danish dictionary.

Amid all these linguistic complications, the trees and plants and flowers and leaves have tranquilly maintained their wordless communication essential for every ceremony and festival, every event, vital or fleeting.

There is a new babel in the world today and men continue to darken counsel by words. Only the flowers which say nothing are understood by all, and there is no speech nor language where their voice is not heard.

A Violet.

God does not send us strange flowers every year.
When the spring winds blow o'er the pleasant places,
The same dear things lift up the same fair faces.
    The violet is here.

It all comes back: the odor, grace and hue;
Each sweet relation of its life repeated,
No blank is left, no looking for is cheated.
    It is the thing we knew.

So after the death-winter it must be.
God will not put strange signs in the heavenly places.
The old love shall look out from the old faces.
    Veilchen! I shall have thee!

MRS. A. D. T. WHITNEY

THE GARDEN IN SHADOW

Violet

VIOLA ODORATA

Across the grass, across the flowers, gently slant the shadows of early morning—ethereal as the fresh dawn which projects them. As the sun mounts higher and pours its rays directly down, the shadows which stretch from the trunks of the trees become denser; those which are dappled by the leaves become sharper. The shrubs gather their penumbra closer to their bases. The flowers pull their slender ghosts erect.

With the sinking of the sun the shadows lengthen, grow fainter, thinner, and gradually fade.

The moon rises and gossamer webs of chiaroscuro slant once more across the grass, across the flowers, unreal as in a radiant dream.

All day, all night, the patterns shift, lengthen, contract. They move with the moving wind; they intensify with the brilliant sunshine.

As the clouds float overhead, their images overlay and then

drift past those of earth, and the shadow of a cloud is like the echo of a voice vibrating far away and yet clear.

Shadows are the charm of a garden. Not only the tracery cast by branches and leaves and flowers, but the well-defined blocks of black—counterparts of the walls of the house, of the roof, of the chimneys; the framed translucence from a lighted window; the path of light from an opened door.

All hours of the day and night, all seasons of the year are thus accompanied. Blue hatchings lie motionless across the winter snow. A leafy screen of violet stippling quivers before a suddenly approaching summer gale.

For this reason landscape architects take care to provide or enhance this sciagraphy of garden design.

Giotto was the first painter to indicate the modeling of the human figure by light and shade; Leonardo the first to note that in nature such contrast is not abrupt but made up of delicate gradations, with the light sliding into the dark and dark creeping into the light, so that what might appear opaque is actually loose and penetrable. Velasquez painted an elastic light illuminating the air with veils of atmosphere. Tintoretto used chiaroscuro as a powerfully dramatic accessory. The action and variation of light and shade give mystery to Rembrandt's canvases and spirituality to Corot's. Turner's experiments in *plein air* made him the leader of the "luminarists."

When we study the pictures of great painters we see how they have translated the crepuscular fluctuations to suggest the real and the imaginary, poetry and emotion. When we look at a lawn or meadow, or at our own small garden in sunshine, at dusk or in starlight, we read the original text without translation.

Sometimes, on a summer night, looking toward the flower beds, I can see, even if there is no moon, the alabaster lilies, the glistening pearl of the foxgloves, the creamy lobes of the peonies. Only white flowers are visible at night. Some of them, like the fraxinella and the nicotiana, give their sweetest fragrance after dewfall. White flowers, shining through the evening, seem those very angels who Vaughan, who held joyful converse with celestial beings, is sure "call to the soul when man doth sleep." At such moments we acknowledge that Vaughan spoke the truth when he added, "So some strange thoughts transcend our wonted themes, and into glory peep . . ."

But sometimes, as we sit there, I do not see angels, or even the little garden which is workaday in sunlight and sublimated in moonlight. I see a lake in Lapland, lying in the magic quietude of the midsummer night.

Encircled by chill mountains and reflecting an undarkening sky, it lies under a forlorn enchantment. Smoother than stretched silk, clearer than liquefied glass, it resigns itself to the laving of the greenish golden light. Even as we sit in our warm, perfumed Virginia garden, the Lapland lake is lying as when we saw it last, in an air of supernal purity. And perhaps at this moment the eclipse of a drifting cloud floats across its tranced and pensive surface, trails away and is gone.

I remember another summer night, when the bay far below Rio de Janeiro had merged into the obscurity of the sky. Above our heads were a thousand, thousand, thousand stars. Below our feet a thousand, thousand lights, like constellations in an inverted heaven, poured down the sides of the mountains, and one tiny spark from a cable car traveled across the void from our starry perch to the top of Sugar Loaf.

I see a ravine in the mountain of Santa Teresa, with houses and shops clinging crazily to its sheer sides, and with a dim street winding along the bottom below. In a small room, with a window open to the air, half a dozen men, their faces illumined by a single light in the center of the table, are playing cards. A shadow passes across the window and the group is eclipsed. A child runs up the street like an insect scampering along a phosphorescent thread.

THE GARDEN IN SHADOW • 127

The deep shade of a high wall falls across her path and she vanishes. Now, for a moment, there are no shadows, only the sound of singing, floating from somewhere through the velvet darkness.

I remember still another place where there were shadows, and I saw this not at night but in the daytime. A low church with a wooden tower stood on a bluff in Switzerland. A river flowed below it and around it lay a garden graveyard, cheerfully planted with flowers. But what made it uniquely tender was that above each grave was a small weeping willow. As I stood looking, a breeze stirred, and each little tree swept a drooping veil back and forth over the grave beneath.

Often when I see a graveyard on a treeless hillside or in an unshielded open plot, I remember the veils of those weeping willows and feel that the garden of the dead would, like the gardens of the living, be lovelier for such implication.

There are other garden shadows than those cast by the sun or the moon or by the lights from the house or the street.

When one who has loved a garden has left it, and it is no longer tended, it seems, even in the brightest day, to be heavy with shadows. Perhaps it is because the trees have not been pruned, or the vines and bushes are overgrown. The grass is so high that it shrouds the strong pushing leaves of the yucca. Honeysuckle weaves a pall over the rosebushes, and mosses have long buried the frailer flowers which once filled the garden beds. Whatever the hour of the day or the season of the year, this gloaming never seems to lift but to grow deeper, so that when you try to trace your way among the beds, they are quite lost, as is the memory of the one who planted them.

But it is possible that some day another owner will come to take possession, and as the secrets of the past are gradually uncovered will find there something that does not exist in a new garden.

It is not so much the tangible survival of growing things as the intangible vibrations which make an old garden wise and mellow. This fleck on the earth's surface has been loved and labored over before, so that love and labor have become an indestructible part of it.

The shadows that shift across it weave an immemorial pattern. Starlight and moonlight and sunshine assume a richer patina because they shine through branches which have spread out their protection through many storms and through the vicissitudes and benedictions of many years.

Now, with the new ownership, the melancholy of grief which was once fresh, and of oblivion that is now old, is dissipated. The expression on the dear familiar face of nature is modeled by the newly risen day and breaks into a smile with the pulsing sun. These are living shadows and, diaphanous as they are, they triumph over the shadows of mortality.

Now elysium, antrum, nemus, paradisus, horties, lucus, etc. signifie all of them *rem sacram et divinam:* for these expedients do influence the soule and spirits of man, and prepare them for converse with good angells.

JOHN EVELYN

A good book is like a garden carried in the pocket.

ARAB PROVERB

PHILOSOPHER IN THE GARDEN

Rose

ROSA

The word garden, which is similar in many languages, means a space set aside for two purposes: the cultivation of certain plants and the cultivation of certain pleasures.

In the United States and northern Europe that pleasure usually includes work and play; in the Orient and southern Europe that pleasure implies meditation and repose.

Such different points of view have quite logically produced different types of gardens.

Perhaps the most obvious difference is the emphasis on privacy. A Chinese garden, a Spanish garden, a garden in Italy, in Mexico, in South or Central America, is so enclosed that it cannot be seen from the street or even from next door. In those countries where labor has always been cheap it has been easy to build high walls of stone; in those countries with tropical climates it is easy to plant hedges which grow rapidly and thickly and are impenetrable to the sight and even to the sound of the outer world.

Because of this concept, the Chinese speak not of planting

but of building a garden, for architecture rather than foliage is the predominating feature. Not only the architecture of the garden but of the house itself.

In most southern and oriental countries, the patio is the central and integral feature of even the humblest home. This word patio has suddenly become prevalent in American speech and is loosely applied to almost any outdoor living space. A patio, actually, is an inner room whose ceiling is open to the sky. It is surrounded on all four sides by the walls of the house, and can be reached from the street only by passing through a door which can be, and usually is, firmly bolted. The eaves of the house are so deep that they overhang and make a roof over the galleries or colonnades, corridors or loggias. Unlike a porch or veranda or terrace, such a corridor is open to outdoors—open to the patio in this instance—on one side only. Thus, it is completely protected from the weather, and can be furnished with permanent chairs and tables, even with lamps and books and pictures and rugs or matting. There may be several patios, each serving a different purpose, but all of them are similar in being invisible from the street and in being inaccessible unless their entrance door or gate is opened.

Patios differ in their size, furnishings and plantings, just as rooms differ in their arrangement and decoration. But whether they have a fountain or a shade tree in the center, a wall fountain or a wall garden on one side, they overcome the feeling of restriction and confinement by avoiding crowding. Trees and vines are often espaliered, so that the foliage does not completely hide the tracery of their trunks and stems against the wall. If there is no space for flower beds or borders, a few potted plants placed at effective points give accent and softness. Glazed and vivid tiles incorporated around the fountain or in benches or in the walls, contribute color.

The true patio is not likely to be generally popular in the

United States. It is not integral to our architecture or to our temperament. The walled garden, however, is more and more often found, and while these have architectural connection with the house, they permit wider and freer outdoor space while still preserving privacy.

In Mexico, which is our nearest foreign neighbor, one may step from the house into a garden with walls eight or ten feet high. Sometimes these are pierced by tiny barred windows, with perhaps a bench built below, so that although passers-by cannot see in, the family can see out. Since a garden which is shut in by the walls of the house, or even by its own high free-standing walls, gives no extended view, a little tower may be raised in one corner or even placed on the flat roof of the house itself. Such an airy observation spot, partially open on four sides and roofed with tile, is reached by an outside stair with vines trained up the side.

The Mirador of Spain, the Belvedere of Italy, the old-fashioned cupola or captain's walk of New England, overlooking the bay, were such retreats, offering a view beyond the garden walls, catching whatever breeze was stirring and protected from sun and wind.

In a patio, in a walled garden, seclusion is the chief objective. Flowers and foliage—indeed, planting of any sort—are incidental. In this country, many people refer to a bed of flowers as a garden, forgetting that there are gardens which have no flowers at all. In a Chinese garden, the principal feature may be a curiously shaped rock, or several rocks, which are placed and valued, not as a background for flower planting but for their own intrinsic beauty and symbolism. Such a rock is a permanent feature and worthy of protection and admiration, while flowers, which are ephemeral, are kept to the courtyards to be cared for by the women.

There are other gardens without flowers, but not without greenery. The Japanese learned from the Chinese the value of masses and open spaces, and the charm of a succession of green, and long after the Chinese had obscured the simplicity of their gardens by over-ornamentation, the Japanese kept to the austere and subtle effects of sparse planting.

The tranquillity of a green garden is coming into greater appreciation in this country. Its interest and charm depend upon the color and texture and form of the leaves and the habits of the plants themselves. Its peaks of intensity are lower than those in the flower garden, and the intervals between them are longer, but the succession of subtle harmonies is unbroken, so that it is a serene sanctuary throughout the year.

There are still other gardens where, owing to the taste of the owner or the exigencies of climate, terrain or exposure, there is no grass, but violets, sedums and ivy are used as ground-covers, and cotyledon and echeverias are clipped to simulate grass. Even such low-growing plants are not essential. Pebbles—black and white, red, yellow and emerald—serve the same purpose and the colorful effect is heightened by paths of intricately laid paving, or even by white sand, kept freshly patterned by sweeping.

Dorothy Graham describes the pavements of the Ming Gardens as set with small gray pebbles, which are a mosaic background for figures of buds and flowers, or for abstract designs. Bricks are set in blocks of five to make alternate squares and placed at an angle to give a herringbone effect.

I remember well a garden overlooking the blue Strait of Juan de Fuca, in Victoria, on Vancouver Island. A slope of gray rock sweeps up from the water, its dim mass and antique structure set in a delicate filigree of choicest planting. Each tree and shrub, each plant and flower, each grouping, is a subordinate part of the total design. The slope of rock, its cleft patterns indicated by restrained verdure, is the matrix. The accents of color and the pattern of growing textures are regulated to enhance that matrix. Here are tiny azaleas and rhododendrons with two-inch blooms. Here are miniature bulbs, bearing flowers no larger than a fingernail. Every month of the year in the soft climate there are heathers of softly muted tints and the tiny stars of saxifrages. At intervals, selected with discrimination, the mosaic mural is picked out by gold or white or violet bloom. The shrubs and trees are trained to the desired shape and angle and stringently pruned to keep them in scale. Thus, the gardener has persuaded a weeping spruce to lie along the edge of a slope and droop over it. From the mountains she brought a two-inch juniper, planted it in a crevice with a thimbleful of sand and a trickle of water; watchfully she pruned it and picked off its seeds and measured its nourishment so that now, on the predetermined spot, there stands a mature and rugged juniper tree, fifteen inches high, precisely and perfectly right in size and character for the precise and perfect position.

This garden is not its flowers, or even the shrubs and trees. It is the actual rock, and the planting exists only to enhance the form and texture.

People who study other gardens than their own often find their tastes changing with the years. Where once we wanted roses clambering over the front door and clematis flinging its tangled mantle across the porch and hollyhocks crowding beside the steps, we may now want quietness, space and composure. We may want an open foreground between us and our flower beds. We may even banish the flowers to a cutting plot, as the Chinese banish them to a secluded courtyard, and leave our garden an enclosure of tranquillity.

How can we picture to ourselves the gardens of this world without seeing them as enclosures? We see the primitive husbandman driving in stakes and weaving boughs between them to keep out thieves and wild animals. We see the people of the ancient East—Egyptian, Babylonian and Assyrian potentates—looking down on their toiling slaves as they labor to raise the massive walls which will shut out the sound and smell of the poverty-stricken multitudes, pressing uncomfortably close. We see the small retreats of the Persians, like precious jewels, in settings cunningly designed to keep out sandstorms, and the vast acreages of nobles in India secured by castellated walls with four large entrance gates. We see the invading Romans settling in England and building garden walls of stone or planting hedges of box such as they knew at home. We see the gardens of Chaucer "walled wel with hye walles embatailled" and those of Shakespeare's time "circummured with brick" or "encompassed on all four sides with stately arched hedges." Those hedges, usually of holly or hornbeam, boasted impregnability, and Evelyn mentions his as being "about four hundred feet in length, nine high and five feet in diameter." It is paradoxical that our generation, which is assured of a longer life span than Elizabeth's and is assisted and speeded on all sides by labor-saving and time-saving devices, rarely has the patience to plant a hedge which will take a dozen years to reach maturity. It might take a long time to grow, but it lived a long time, too, and much of the charm of the English countryside is due to the thick and ancient hedges flowering in the spring and green in the snows of winter.

We range farther in our mind's eye and see the missionary monks from Europe, spreading from South to North to South America, and wherever they placed a mission, planting their medicinal and culinary herbs in one enclosure and the flowers to decorate the church in another.

We see the early colonists of this country contriving their heavy stockades against the Indians, and later the farmers clearing their fields and piling the rocks into those stone boundaries which are still characteristic of our East, or cutting and splitting and placing the rails for those fences which were characteristic of the northern Middle West.

From earliest history the wall has been symbolic of the garden and its destruction implied the destruction of the garden itself, as when Isaiah says, "And now I will tell you what I will do with my vineyard: I will take away the hedge thereof and it shall be eaten up: I will break down the wall thereof, and it shall be trodden down."

As we go on with our dreaming and recall the gardens of our world today, we see white picket fences in New England surrounding old-fashioned vegetable and flower beds, and the box hedges of Virginia patterning the lawns. In the semitropical regions boundary lines which were marked off by bare posts have sprouted green leaves like Aaron's rod and almost as quickly. It is always affecting to me to see what looked like dead wood returning to the kingdom of the living, and avocados ripening amid thickly interwoven branches.

It would seem that in most parts of the world it is more necessary to have a wall outside a garden than flowers inside, and this tradition of unnumbered centuries still persists even when we no longer need a barrier against attacking enemies or marauding beasts.

When we read of philosophers who passed their days in their gardens, we inevitably picture these as gardens enclosed.

The philosophers may or may not have been surrounded by flower beds and borders, but they were most certainly insured privacy by walls. It was in such fresh and fragrant seclusion with unobstructed space that they could watch the shadows slanting, deepening, flickering and fading. Here they could see the moonlight lie in long white bands, and from here they could look up at the stars.

Epicurus, it is said, passed his life wholly in his garden, finding his pleasure not in digging and planting but in studying, exercising and teaching. It was the abode which contributed "to both the Tranquillity of Mind and Indolence of the Body which he made his Chief Ends."

Theophrastus also spent his life in his garden. It was a long life, for he lived to be eighty-five. And it must have been a large garden, for at one time two thousand pupils flocked to the Peripatetic School, which Aristotle had founded. After his death, the garden remained the center of the school, with the house and colonnades, all of which he bequeathed to it. He hoped his friends would still foregather there and that his old gardener would continue his services, and he stipulated that his own bones should repose there.

The gardens of Solomon were planted with all sorts of fruit trees and watered with fountains. "Although we have no more particular descriptions of them, yet we may find they were the places where he passed the times of his leisure and delight with those of his wives that he loved the best." Indeed, Paradise, which seems to be a Persian word, meant originally merely an enclosed space set apart and adorned with trees.

One does not have to be a philosopher or a king to enjoy the "Sweetness of Air, the Pleasantness of Smells, the Verdure of Plants" . . . "The Exemption from Cares and Sollicitude, seem equally to favour and improve, both Contemplation and Health, the Enjoyment of Sense and Imagination, and thereby the Quiet and Ease both of the Body and Mind."

These are the most valued fruits of any garden, but the meditative mind seems inclined toward those which are unconfused by too great profusion of planting.

A garden in which the owner spends much time becomes a reflector of his temperament, so that it might be argued that our moods, quite as much as our minds, determine the type of our garden.

Happily, there is room for every type on our terrestrial world. Room for beds of the gay and impatient annuals which press upon each other's heels, so fast they come and so eager are they to scatter their seeds and be gone. Room for the majestic perennials which may outlive the hands which planted them. There is room for whole hillsides of jonquils, and whole acres of tulips, and immense

lantations of gladioli, although these belong in the province of
the nurseryman or the horticulturist, who is chiefly interested in
numbers and varieties of species. There is room for gardens which
share their cheerful show with every passer-by and for those which
enclose themselves and their owners in privacy. Room for the
glorious displays of the very rich who engage professionals to take
over the business. Room for the little plots of the poor, who sacrifice time and space from practical necessities to plant and care for
a few flowers. Room for public gardens which everyone may see.
Room for green gardens without flowers and for wild gardens without discipline.

To each of these, those who love them bring their willing
labors and offer their spoken or unspoken praise. From them we
take living pleasure and in them we leave our mundane cares and
even our deeper griefs.

Thus it is that a garden gradually becomes a repository of
human emotions. As we draw from it our comfort, so does it draw
from us its inward and outward character.

Anyone can copy a garden and, by taking thought, can
choose a handsome model. But whether we choose or not, if we so
much as lay our hand upon it, we create our own particular garden.
That my garden is imperfect, I am well aware. But it has a wall
on three sides and its fourth side is the house. Perhaps I do not
perceive all of its defects because when I look at it I see it not
as it is, but as it will be next year—the year after that—the year
after that . . .

It exists within its confines like a small cartouch for a large
map not yet drawn, and I sometimes dare to hope it indicates the
perfect one I may be permitted to make and tend in Paradise.

An old lady's advice on choosing a gardener: "Look at his trousers. If they're patched in the knees, you want him; if they're patched in the seat, you don't."

FARMER'S JOURNAL, BELFAST

A GARDEN IS A GARDEN

Petunia

PETUNIA HYBRIDA

Americans, who seem to prefer to make discoveries not singly but en masse, have discovered the pleasures of living outdoors.

Terraces or patios opening out of living or dining rooms, a fireplace or barbecue built in the back or side yard are now incorporated into a majority of the new houses being planned, and only await a let-up in building restrictions to be added to old houses. Outdoor tables and chairs and hurricane lamps and movable bars and huge adjustable umbrellas are enjoying a record sale.

This certainly is one of the most delightful improvements in homemaking since Noah built the Ark. It cannot be too highly commended, although it is singular that the American public has taken so long to adopt a practical and happy idea which has been in use in Europe for centuries.

I have, however, one small protest to offer—a protest which will not and should not affect the popularity of this excellent trend, but which may stir a sympathetic echo from some kindred reader. This is the lightly tossed off injunction, "Make your garden into an outdoor room." An eminent landscape gardener has positively announced, "Arrange your garden according to the same principles you use in arranging your living room. Consider the general effect you want, the colors, the varying heights of shrubs and flowers as you do the varying colors, bulk and heights of furniture in a room."

I lift my voice to denounce such advice, except for that fractional minority who possess greenhouses which can constantly replenish bare or flowerless or straggly spots, and who are able to hire gardeners who can transplant all things at all seasons.

When you re-cover an armchair in pale rose brocade and put it in a certain place, it stays in that place and retains its size and contribution to the general color scheme until you move it or re-cover it. When you cross the threshold some fine morning you are not confronted with a dozen miniature armchairs sprouting up everywhere, and the original article deepened to a hateful and unnegotiable magenta.

But when you plant a bed of blue and white petunias and sally forth the following spring, you may find purplish blue petunias all over the place and never a white one visible. You build in a radio cabinet, and put it where you want it, and there it is for keeps. But you plant a few peonies and, before you know it, you have burgeoning mountains of peonies crowding out everything else. You plant a few perennial ageratums or Michaelmas daisies, and—oh well, you know . . .

The carefully spaced lilies in my small plot walk about wherever they please, and so, for that matter, do the columbines. It is as disconcerting as if the pictures in my bedroom changed places, multiplied, took to themselves wings and disappeared entirely, and then possibly reappeared in the pantry.

You may, unfortunately, find moths in your davenport and,

even more unfortunately, termites in your baseboard. But you do not find thrips and aphids, beetles, mildew, blight and moles attacking the legs of your tables and chairs. A water pipe may burst and damage your ceiling, but there is no danger of an early frost withering your lamp shades, or a violent rain beating the books from their shelves and battering them into the mud.

No one who enjoys working in a garden objects to the exigencies of nature or to this curious willfulness of flowers to take the altering of their hues or habitat into their own hands. We rearrange and discard and try again, and although we have to wait for another year to be sure of the effect, we do not grudge the time, for that time is always in the future, and therefore we always have two gardens—the present one and the potential one.

But we do object to the airy assumption that the garden is just another room. In the house we take down the winter draperies and put up summer ones and mitigate the darkness of the velvet upholstery by cool slip covers. This is the only definite alteration required. But in a garden we must put the spring bulbs where they will not conflict with the summer bloom, and arrange them all so there will be space for the flowers of autumn.

If a garden must be compared with a room, that room would be a combination laboratory, cellar, mortuary and chamber in Paradise.

But why compare it to a room? Why compare it to anything? Why not consider it for what it is—a garden, with all its problems and never-ceasing demand upon our care, and joy to our eyes and hearts?

Gertrude Stein made one statement which is comprehensible even to a layman when she wrote, "A rose is a rose is a rose." Let us defy the false chant that a garden is an outdoor room, and stubbornly whisper, partly in exasperation and partly in loving pride, "A garden is a garden is a garden."

Four Seasons fill the measure of the year;
 There are four seasons in the mind of man:
He has his lusty Spring, when fancy clear
 Takes in all beauty with an easy span:
He has his Summer, when luxuriously
 Spring's honey'd cud of youthful thought he loves
To ruminate, and by such dreaming high
 Is nearest unto Heaven: quiet coves
His soul has in its Autumn, when his wings
 He furleth close; contented so to look
On mists in idleness—to let fair things
 Pass by unheeded as a threshold brook:
He has his Winter too of pale misfeature,
Or else he would forego his mortal nature.

KEATS

SEASON'S GREETINGS

Iris

IRIS PSEUDACORUS

Once upon a time, and not so long ago, the seasons were marked by special delicacies available only at that time. We had June peas in June, fresh corn in July and August, spring lamb in the spring, turkey at Thanksgiving and salmon made its first appearance on the Fourth of July. Oysters were confined to the months with an R, and Brazil nuts, English walnuts and almonds were initially greeted at Christmas.

All that is changed. With the new methods of quick-freezing and improved transportation by rail and air, practically all edibles are at our disposal the whole year through, and fragile tropical fruits are flown from the sunshine of the far South to the snow-blanketed shops of the North.

To be sure, our great-grandmothers put up fruits and vegetables. They dried apples, stored root crops, canned tomatoes and beans, and filled jars and bottles with pickles. But neither in variety nor excellence could these compare with present-day products, frozen almost as soon as they are picked, packed and expressed in refrigerated cars or ships, or borne in a few hours through the air from their native habitat.

The modern child and the young housewife would find it hard to distinguish between February and September if they reckoned the seasons by kitchen and dining room. We may eat lettuce and strawberries, broiled spring chicken and new potatoes the year round.

This expansion of the daily menu is a consummation devoutly to be praised, and perhaps as we munch a cherimoya or a sapodilla from Guatemala and, as the Guatemalans eat apples from the United States, our mutual appreciation of one another will expand correspondingly.

For hundreds of years food has created trade routes, stimulated commerce, influenced international relations and even affected languages. The simple commodity of salt, for instance, is responsible for ancient roads hundreds of miles long, and charted lanes over the seas, known as salt routes, since they were used chiefly for bringing salt to countries where it could not be obtained from either mines or sea water. Every Roman soldier was given regularly a small amount of money for buying salt. The Latin word for salt is sal, and this money was called a salarium, which means salt money. From it our word salary has come.

I cannot detect a single fault in the admirable and ever-increasing exchange of foods between different regions, bringing with it better meals, better health and better trade relations.

But we should, perhaps, be grateful that in this world of commutations and permutations there remain some fixed factors, so we can keep our balance in regard to geography and the calendar.

For despite the most scientific systems of irrigation, men do not raise pineapples on the Canadian mountains or celery in the jungles of Panama. Despite central heating in winter and air conditioning in summer, there is yearly snowfall in the temperate and

igid zones, and heat along the lowlands of the equator for twelve
nbroken months.

If our imaginations do not range over such a vast survey of
errain, we can maintain a sense of proportion and stability by
merely looking out of our windows or, best of all, by cultivating
ur gardens.

For our small domestic plots are as yet unaffected by this
particular march of progress. Crocuses refuse to unfurl in August.
Delphiniums do not flourish in a climate that is too hot, and crape
myrtle will not winter in the far North.

When we work in our gardens we are still working amid the
natural elements. We must reckon with the probabilities of frost
and rainfall, and scurry to get our seeds in as soon as the ground is
ready and to pick the last flowers before they are nipped by cold.

These processes, which are familiar to every gardener, no
matter how unpretentious, are rationalizers. They make the seasons
vivid and remind us constantly of the blessings of sunshine and the
threat of gales.

If we are amateurs, we soon learn to leave to professional
horticulturists the task of raising violets in midwinter and cutting
long-stemmed roses when the eaves of the greenhouse are hung
with icicles. If we move from one location to another we learn, too
—if we are wise—not to attempt the impossible or even the too
difficult.

While our immediate climatic environment may heighten
certain nostalgic longings, it may also heighten our wonder at certain universalities. I have seen bright-faced impatiens sparkling in
Argentina and in Canada, just as it sparkles in my own garden,
and my heart leaped in recognition.

I have seen iris in Japan and marigolds in Africa, and wel-
comed these well-known forms as the mariner or the astronomer
welcomes familiar planets and constellations in the skies.

I rejoice at the scientific advance which has made it possible for us to open in Oregon a box containing a lei of swooningly sweet ginger blossoms which were growing in Honolulu the day before, and in Vermont to open a florist box where carnations rest on ferns flown from Oregon. I acknowledge these things with my mind, but I greet with a special upsurge of feeling the first snowdrop which dares to shine by my own doorstep, not too early, not too late, and the last chrysanthemum which holds its brave head against the first impact of winter.

Except for nature's inexorable insistence upon the cycle of seasons, we would be in danger of losing all cosmic perspective. It is the fashion for Christmas carols to be heard in the streets and in shops not only for weeks before Christmas, but we may, if we wish, listen to a record of Handel's *Messiah* on the hottest day of July, since music, like other commodities, is now canned.

But our gardens will remind us that the earth still creates its various soils, and the weather reminds us that nature still has her immemorial successions. The Christmas star shines according to celestial laws regardless of advertising slogans.

We acknowledge with humbleness that there is one glory of the summer and one glory of the autumn and another of the winter and of spring. And each season differeth from another in glory.

I found the poems in the fields
And only wrote them down.

JOHN CLARE

The narrow bud opens her beauties to
The sun, and love runs in her thrilling veins.

WILLIAM BLAKE

See the young lilies, their scymitar petals
Glancing like silver 'mid earthier metals:
Dews of the brightest in life-giving showers
Fall all the night on these luminous flowers.
Each of them sparkles afar like a gem.
Wouldst thou be smiling and happy like them?
O, follow all counsel that Pleasure proposes;
It dies, it flies, the Time of the Roses!

JAMES CLARENCE MANGAN

They Are Not Long.
> *Vitae summa brevis spem nos vetat inchoare
> longam.*

They are not long, the weeping and the laughter,
    Love and desire and hate:
I think they have no portion in us after
    We pass the gate.

They are not long, the days of wine and roses:
    Out of a misty dream
Our path emerges for a while, then closes
    Within a dream.

ERNEST DOWSON

FOUR POETS AND FOUR GARDENS

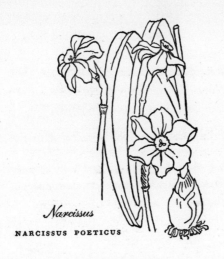

Narcissus

NARCISSUS POETICUS

The poets have a good deal to answer for when it comes to any discussion of flowers and nature in general.

Until fairly recently many of them were inclined to consider roses and lilies, rosemary and rue, chiefly for the music of their syllables. There is certainly no objection to their referring to the asphodel as if it were the flower of dreams instead of the bright-faced narcissus, and they are not to be censured if they choose to call an ailanthus the Tree of Heaven. In fact, that fashion—if sometimes a bit shaky, botanically speaking—has some advantages over the present one which prefers to call the ailanthus the stink-wood.

To be sure, among the poets who are vague, and those who are unduly delicate, or those who are determinedly ugly, there are hundreds whose exquisitely precise floral references and similes are truer than the most painstakingly literal botanical descriptions, so that whole books are compiled of such rhymed tributes. In fact, there are so many such verses that it is difficult to write anything about gardens and not be tempted to include more quotations than original text.

But there is one poet who is not often quoted, whose name is not even generally known, but who, more than any other, spoke not so much as an observer of the growing world, but almost as if that world were speaking through him.

This is John Clare, who was born the son of a pauper farmer in Helston, England, in 1793 and died in 1864, after having been confined for twenty-seven years in a madhouse.

We know how John Clare looked—small of stature, with wide eager eyes and a high forehead and long light hair falling down in wild tangles to his shoulders. He is in the poorest sort of peasant smock, and his hands are the unkempt scarred hands of a field laborer. He bows as he is introduced into your polite society awkwardly, but with a proper deference, showing that he accepts your position and his own. Although he has been up to London once, in a borrowed overcoat to cover his stained smock frock; although he has met Lamb and Hood, Coleridge, Hazlitt and De Quincey; although Madame Vestris has recited at Covent Garden one of the verses from his newly published volume, and Rossini has set another to music, he is uncomplainingly aware that he is the son of a pauper farmer. But it is not the irrevocable humbleness of his lot that has brought the look of defeat into his agonized, sensitive face. No, in 1820 in England one accepts the stratum of one's birth as one accepts blue eyes or brown. It is the strain of physical overwork, of continual undernourishment, the terror and pressure of a domestic load too heavy for him to support, that is already casting a shadow of derangement across his face. He is only twenty-seven, and he has two aged parents, his wife and a rapidly increasing family to maintain, as an unskilled laborer. They all live in the wretched hut in which he himself was born. This, then, is John Clare, England's "peasant poet," for whom Mr. Taylor, his bland publisher, introducing his first volume, apologizes: "And although Poets in this country have seldom been fortunate men, yet he is, perhaps, the least favored by circumstances and the most destitute of friends of any who ever existed."

Mr. Taylor has not overstated the case. John Clare, who knows every flower and weed and bird and insect of his native fields so well that his poems are not descriptions of reality so much as reality itself, loves them with such passionate and intimate completeness that he not infrequently forgets that there are human beings in the world. "Man I never did like, and woman has long since sickened me," he wrote later in a letter to Dr. Allen. But the "white-nosed bee," the "little chumbling mouse gnarling the dead weeds for her house," the first sunbeam on the stream "split by the willows wavy grey," the solitary crane winging lonely to the unfrozen dykes,

> *Cranking a jarring melancholy cry*
> *Through the wild journey of the cheerless sky,*

the baby blackbirds caught by a sudden shower

> *. . . in a nest of love*
> *Where the hedge the bramble hopples*
> *Cried, cawed and stretched their necks above*
> *With their down all hung with dropples,*

into these sounds and sights he has transfused his very soul. Never before nor since, in the history of English letters, has this peculiar merging of human consciousness been emotionalized with such delicate ardor or sung with such utter simplicity.

He watches insects—those "tiny loiterers on the barley's beard," "smoothing the velvet of the pale hedge-rose," not as a scientist watches, deliberately, collecting facts; not as the moralist watches, seeking to find a lesson. He simply sees and loves the actual incidents of the actual fields, in his own particular part of

England. He does not even select his material. He enumerates caressingly, beginning anywhere and stopping anywhere.

> *Crimp-filled daisy, bright bronze buttercup*
> *Freckt cowslip peeps, gilt whins of morning dew.*

He does not strive to be poetic or original. He merely recounts his loves, with naïve and unforgettable exactitude.

> *No matter how the world approved,*
> *'Twas nature listened, I that loved,*

he says.

The result of his exquisitely objective adoration is one of curious reality, and a handful of songs beyond all criticism because they are, in their own peculiar métier, unsurpassed.

John Clare's early work was written during intervals between sheep-tending, gardening, working in a lime-kiln and ditching in the fields. The hut in which he was born, according to his biographer, Frederick Martin, "was narrow and wretched, more like a prison than a human dwelling; and the hut stood in a dark gloomy plain covered with stagnant pools of water and overhung by mists during the greater part of the year."

His father was dependent on parish relief and the family existed chiefly on potatoes and water gruel. When Clare was seven, he was sent to look after the sheep and geese on the heath, and at twelve was put to work in the fields.

This is the time of which he writes:

> *For everything I felt a love*
> *The weeds below, the birds above*
> *And weeds that bloomed in summer's hours*
> *I thought they should be reckoned flowers.*
> *They made a garden free for all*
> *And so I loved them great and small*

> *. . . Until I even danced for joy*
> *A happy and a lonely boy.*

When Clare's broken and prematurely aged body was incarcerated, his lyrical faculty was simultaneously liberated. A new joy springs into his verse. The conflict is over. He need no longer sorrow for his lost human love, or contend with overwhelming human difficulties. In the "silken bed and roomy painted hall" of his madness, he can watch the

> *. . . little lambtoe bunches springs*
> *In red tinged and begolden dye*
> *Forever, and like China kings*
> *They come, but never seem to die.*

He can lie, with his head on a cushion of moss, and muse that on such a velvet seat David sat and played his harp.

> *And David's crown has passed away*
> *Yet poesy breathes his shepherd's skill*
> *His palace lost, and to this day,*
> *The little moss is blooming still.*

He has become a child again. His enfeebled body with its large head bowed over in the attitude of habitual thought is that of a broken field laborer, but his limpid soul is flowing into the stream of nature all around him, and is reflecting her beloved face. Once again he is the child who cries:

> *The cowslips on the meadow lea*
> *How have I run for them!*
> *I looked with wild and childish glee*
> *Upon each golden gem.*
> *And when they bowed their heads so shy*
> *I laughed, and thought they danced for joy.*

The springtime of the year and the springtime of the race fuse in his mind. About the child who

> . . . could not die when fields were green.
> For he loved the time too well,

he exclaims wonderingly:

> Infants, the children of the Spring!
>   How can an infant die
> When butterflies are on the wing,
>   Green grass, and such a sky—
> How can they die at spring?

The spring of 1837 brings madness to John Clare. And madness brings release. Except for brief periods of melancholy when he remembers

> I am a sad and lonely hind.
> Trees tell me so, day after day,
> As slowly they wave in the wind,

he is gently content. He sits in a sunny alcove reading, or lies on the grass, watching the bees "stroke their little legs across their wings," and listening to "the water ruckling into waves." It is here that he writes the final sublime lines which are included in every anthology of English poetry, and by which he is chiefly remembered by the casual reader, those lines ending

> I long for scenes where man has never trod,
> A place where women never smiled or wept;
> There to abide with my creator GOD
> And sleep as I in childhood gently slept,
> Untroubling and untroubled where I lie
> The grass below—above, the vaulted sky.

Nature, to John Clare, is not a symbol of anything else. It is the supreme and satisfying reality, and into this fragrant and absorbing reality he enters, as he leaves the world of men.

It was a quite different reality in which another poet lived so long. William Blake's birth was humble, his life was a close and continual struggle with poverty, and he wrote enchantingly of lambs and roses and "honied dew" and he was and still is considered quite mad by the majority of people. But the skyey madness that illuminated William Blake was different from the cloud which shut off John Clare from his fellows, just as Blake's "lillies by the water fair" are of quite different texture and scent from John Clare's primrose "with its crimped and curdled leaf."

Blake was city born and city bred. With the exception of three years at Felpham and for occasional walks in the country with his beloved Kate—his "shadow of delight"—his human habitation was bound by the cramped yard in the rear of his house in the Hercules Buildings. But his human habitation was the least thing that interested William Blake. He could at any time, to use his own words, "enter into Noah's rainbow and make a friend and a companion of one of these images of wonder which always entreat him to leave mortal things."

Living in one small room in which he and his wife ate, and slept, and together worked at his engraving and printing, he was continually surrounded by an innumerable host of angels singing "Everything that lives is holy," of tender lambs in "clothing of delight," of lions with "ruddy eyes that flow with tears of gold." He saw these animals and flowers as clearly as John Clare saw his —for, as he explained: "Man's perceptions are not bounded by organs of perception. He perceives more than sense (though ever so acute) can discover." For one who believes "The imagination is not a State: it is the Human Existence itself," or in even more metaphysical terms, "Imagination is the Divine Body of the Lord Jesus, blessed forever," it is inevitable that all temporal objects should be merely symbols of eternal truths. Thus when Blake writes that

> *Monks in Black gowns*
> *Were walking in the grounds*
> *And binding with briars*
> *My joys and desires,*

he is not referring to any sharp and actual brier like the one that bit John Clare's roughened fingers, but to a thorny symbol of man's harsh prohibitions. When he writes of the lamb and the cloud and the tiger and the clod, he uses them quite simply as illustrations of divine attributes. He observes as vividly and naïvely as Clare, but his perceptions are, as he expresses it, "through the eye, not with it." He delineates what he sees with the same concrete exactitude, but what he sees is the essence.

> *For double the vision my eyes do see,*
> *And a double vision is always with me.*
> *With my inward eye 'tis an old man gray*
> *With my outward a thistle across my way.*

Not that Blake himself is a moralist. The moralist is concerned with good and evil, right and wrong conduct. Blake is far beyond that entire region of thought. It is *being*, not *action*, that interests him. He does not worship good or condemn evil. He worships energy, the parent fire of life, "because the soul of sweet delight can never be defil'd." His poetry is a clear and passionate affirmation of that sublime, that God-intoxicated energy. It expresses itself in "the ruddy limbs and flaming hair" of youth, in the "lily white that shall love delight," and in the unveiling of the naked soul. What he says of his painting could be as well applied to his poetry. "But as I cannot paint Dirty rags and old Shoes where I ought to place Naked Beauty or simple ornament, I despair of ever pleasing one Class of Men."

Like the great parables, the best of Blake's poetry, the lyrics, may be read by a child or a philosopher.

> *If the sun and moon should doubt*
> *They'd immediately go out*

may be regarded as a nursery couplet or as a truth of more possible significance than the Einstein theory. ("God forbid," he said, "that truth should be confined to mathematical demonstration. He who does not know truth at sight is not worthy of her notice.") For those who choose to hold to the nursery couplet interpretation, naturally Blake is merely a silly old gaffer.

The spring that comes to such a soul as this is necessarily a rapturous spiritual manifestation rather than a natural phenomenon.

> *Such pleasure as the teeming earth*
> *Doth take in easy nature's birth*
> *When she puts forth the life of everything;*
> *And in a dew of sweetest rain*
> *She lies delivered without pain*
> *Of the prime beauty of the year, the spring.*

We do not expect too explicit descriptions of earthly plants and flowers from a man who speaks quite casually of God "putting his head to the window," who gently insists that he frequently sees and converses with Dante, Voltaire, Jesus Christ and Milton, who says, "I write when commanded by the spirits, and the moment I have written I see the words fly about the room in all directions. It is then published and the spirits can read."

He writes in a letter to a friend: "I am more famed in Heaven for my works than I could well conceive. In my brain are studies and chambers filled with books and pictures of old, which I wrote and painted in ages of eternity before my mortal life; and those works are the delight and study of archangels." He who utters such wild rhapsodies will be classified by the critics, both of his day and ours, as "an insane man of genius." His friend called him "the gentle visionary Blake." Even his faithful wife occasionally complained that "Mr. Blake was incessantly away in Paradise."

A fiery ecstasy of imagination, an oblivion to worldly things, an absorption in the inner life of the mind and an absolutely literal belief in those things which all Christians profess to believe, created a garden whose flowers were never seen on earth. To live in barest poverty and to declare "I want for nothing" and to die singing are not the usual characteristics of a dirt farmer. The springtime that Blake celebrates in his *Songs of Innocence* is not the springtime that we know or that John Clare knew. It is the Springtime from on High, revealed only to those "gentle souls who guide the great wine-press of Love."

How comes the spring to another mad poet? The Irish spring, tender and mystic? The breeze that is ruffling the grasses about John Clare's feet, this selfsame breeze, tainted with dust from Dublin streets and odors from Dublin gutters, is eddying around a strange gliding figure, wholly oblivious to its touch. Who is this man in a tight threadbare coat buttoned closely up to his chin, a quaint, crazy, steeple-shaped hat like a witch's and with umbrella clutched under his arm? His delicate face is corpselike, the intellectual features withered, the fine hair bleached almost white. Only his eyes, extraordinarily blue and glittering, proclaim his vitality.

He darts into an open door, that of the University of Dublin, and as we follow him we remember the brief outlines of his history. Born into poverty thirty wretched years ago, he has been a copyist in a scrivener's office for seven weary years. He has been an attorney's clerk; with very little education, and a mother and sister to support, he has contributed to the Irish magazines and Penny Journals—never to British publications, being a passionate Papist and a rebel—and has somehow managed to teach himself many foreign languages and acquire an extensive and peculiar culture. At last, given employment in the University Library at Dublin, he spends all his spare hours where we shall now find him, perched specterlike on the top of a ladder in some recess of the building, a large book in his arms, and his soul in the book.

How comes the spring to this strange abstracted scholar? It comes as winter comes, as summer comes. Without joy, without hope. He who has longed to travel and has never left Ireland nor ever will, he who loves the country and has never been farther than the hills of Wicklow, has chartered other passage to other realms. His only travels are those in which, with the aid of his blessed opium, he drifts away entirely from the purgatory of earth, in strange wild voyages whose return is agony.

> And visions of all brilliant hues
> Lap my lost soul in gladness
> Until I awake again
> And the dark lava-fires of madness
> Once more sweep through my brain.

What is there about this obscure eccentric with his pallid face, sitting high on a ladder, devouring an ancient Spanish tome, that has become so inextricably fused with English poetry? Not his wretchedness. Fearful as his sufferings have been and are destined to be, suffering alone does not entitle one to immortality. Not his polyglot culture, remarkable as that is. But the luxuriance and beauty of the dream-world in which he lives, and the undefiled sweetness of his nature. Beaten by circumstances which were too much for his peculiar temperament, James Clarence Mangan was wrecked in health and morale by the time he was thirty. From then until he died at forty-six, his material existence was nothing but a torturing treadmill of life-in-death, and he was always humble, affectionate and prayerful. He never envied others their good fortune, or blamed his own lack of it on anyone but himself. He died apologizing for the trouble he was making.

The reader may find it all in his poetry: the physical misery, the mental versatility, the spiritual sensitiveness <u>and the poetic</u> facility. He will find these things in the fervidly patriotic ballads of Ireland which have always kept Mangan dear to Irish hearts. He will find them in the "translations" from the Spanish, German, "Coptic," Persian and what-not—"translations" which portray not only Mangan's familiarity with foreign tongues but also his shrewd knowledge that his own verse would command a readier market under such spurious guise. And he will find the record of a terrified and yet undefiant human consciousness enduring the torments of intermittent madness, a record of

> the soul
> The startled soul, upbounding from the mire
> Of earthliness and all alive with fears
> Unsmothered by the lethargy of years.

Unlike Blake and Clare, Mangan was not considered mad by his contemporaries, and he has almost entirely escaped the present-day psychoanalytical critic. Our chief authority for deciding that he was a pathological case is himself. A wild note of derangement tears through all he wrote like a yell.

> I see black dragons mount the sky
> I see earth yawn beneath my feet
> I feel within the asp, the worm,
> That will not sleep and can not die.

"The Groans of Despair," "The Song of a Maniac," "Four Idiot Brothers"—the very titles of these poems are revealing. Everywhere are scattered references to the heart, yearning, "in its lucid moods, To Thee alone"—references to being cruelly robbed of "brains and bread and glory" by the fiend of his own disorder and weakness.

His preoccupation with the subject is more painful because more subjective than even Poe's. In his most powerful ballad, "The Nameless One," he achieves the apotheosis of his art and of his suffering. Here is the supreme terror of demoralized emotion depicted by a powerful mind just about to crack. Like John Clare's "I am," Mangan's "The Nameless One" is in every anthology of English verse. It is a spectacular masterpiece of despair. What kind of a garden could Mangan plant, or even write about? In one of those moments when the poor city-dweller was hurriedly aware that somewhere outside of Dublin's dust and racket there were springtime flowers and the song of birds, he groans:

> But when shall rest be mine? Alas!
> When first the winter wands shall wave
> The pale wild flowers and long dark grass
> Above mine unremembered grave.

He did not know what flowers or what grass. His garden was a drifting figment of imagination.

There is still another poet who wrote about other flowers growing in another garden. In Ernest Dowson's sonnet, "To One in Bedlam," the flowers are wisps of straw.

> With delicate, mad hands, behind his sordid bars,
> Surely he hath his posies, which they tear and twine;
> Those scentless strips of straw, that miserably line
> His strait, caged universe, whereat the dull world stares,
>
> Pedant and pitiful. O, how his rapt gaze wars
> With their stupidity! Know they what dreams divine
> Lift his long, laughing reveries like enchaunted wine,
> And make his melancholy germane to the stars?

O lamentable brother! if those pity thee,
Am I not fain of all thy lone eyes promise me;
Half a fool's kingdom, far from men who sow and reap,
All their days, vanity? Better than mortal flowers,
Thy moon-kissed roses seem: better than love or sleep,
The star-crowned solitude of thine oblivious hours!

The man who wrote this was a figure slighter, frailer, younger than the others. He had none of Clare's worshipful absorption in nature, none of Blake's exaltation, none of Mangan's emotional weight. He was a delicate, shy youth with a look and manner of pathetic charm. His face was that of "an archangel slightly damaged," his voice and gestures exquisitely refined, and his clothes decidedly dilapidated. Ernest Dowson is one of the weaker and yet curiously persistent personalities in the English poetry of the nineties.

While he succeeded in being very completely and very constantly miserable during his thirty-three years of life, this misery was in no way caused by unkind circumstances of birth or of fortune. He was well-educated, although irregularly so. Frequently shabby and even hungry, he was never entirely without funds. Never robust, he had sufficient strength for a normal existence, had he desired one. He wasted them all—his strength, his money and his social opportunities. The only thing that he honored was his art, and for that he had a pure and ambitionless reverence, and, from that ash, has grown the small white immortelle of his remembrance.

Dowson had dallied with hashish in Oxford, but later he concentrated, with a fidelity deserving a worthier mistress, upon alcohol. When sober, he was one of the most charming figures in the literary circle of his day. When drunk, he was an irresponsible madman. More definitely than most alcoholics, more definitely than most poets, he was the victim of dual personality. To the consummately artistic blending of these two divergent consciousnesses, "To One in Bedlam" owes its unique value.

Dowson lacked the intellectual vigor that distinguished Clare and Blake and Mangan. He possessed to an abnormal and intensified degree their sensibility. It was this tortured sensibility that drove him, when his dreams eluded him, into sordid surroundings and grossest human contacts. In England, he lived by preference in a moldering house near an old dock. In Paris, it was Les Halles, and in Dieppe, the squalid harbor dives, that were the haunts of that romantic figure, with his fastidious face, his yearning body and his diction so choice and harmonious that even now, forty-nine years after it has been silent in death, it still echoes in the ears that heard it.

"There was never a simpler or more attaching charm," writes Arthur Symons, who knew him, "because there was never a simpler or more honest nature. It was not because he ever said anything particularly clever or particularly interesting, it was not because he gave you ideas, or impressed you by any strength or originality that you liked to be with him; but because of a certain engaging quality which seemed unconscious of itself, which was never anxious to be or do anything, which simply existed as perfume exists in a flower."

Why do we in America, far away in time and in space, remember this plaintive and picturesque young man? Because, in spring, the oldest poets stir again the embers of their drowsy fires, new poets unfold on every side like violets overnight, and all youth that is not improvising its own verse is quoting some poet's.

During a certain spring a little over fifty years ago, the literati of England and America were avowing in rapt unison

> *I am desolate and sick of an old passion,*
> *Yea, hungry for the lips of my desire:*
> *I have been faithful to thee, Cynara! in my fashion.*

FOUR POETS AND FOUR GARDENS · 165

For one year, for two, even for three, the intoxicating lines were chanted, and Dowson's delicate features and demoralized existence became a fetish. And even now, through the roar of violent modern free verse, the clamor of new voices, and the resuscitation of old, there still persists the note of his fluid and reticent song.

> *I have forgot much, Cynara! gone with the wind,*
> *Flung roses, roses riotously with the throng,*
> *Dancing, to put thy pale, lost lilies out of mind;*
> *But I was desolate and sick of an old passion,*
>   *Yea, all the time, because the dance was long:*
> *I have been faithful to thee, Cynara! in my fashion.*

As a patch of ephemeral bright flowers will suddenly every spring brush the side of an immemorial hill, in the selfsame spot, and with the selfsame fleeting enchantment, so always every spring there will be new discoveries of Cynara.

Dowson was not a lover or even an observer of Nature. She was for him only a dreamy symbol of sentiment. "No roses are pale enough for me," he sighs. But he is a poet of springtime, because he is a poet of youth. His misery is of exquisite unsubstantiality, just as his squalor is a perversion of refinement.

Clare's flowers were actual flowers so real one feels the texture of their petals and their leaves. His flowers "sleep within their hoods." His daisies "button into buds." Blake's were mystical symbols, Mangan's were only poor sapless things, growing occasionally from the rich turmoil of his mind, and Dowson's garden was a playground for his fancy.

He belongs with the other three because he was, in his frail fashion, a pure poet; because he was kin to those in whose blood madness flies, and because he is bound by the most impalpable of threads to the enduring poetry of those flowers which bloom only in the spring.

Through primrose tufts, in that green bower,
The periwinkle trailed its wreaths;
And 'tis my faith that every flower
Enjoys the air it breathes.

WORDSWORTH

THE FIRST GARDEN AND THE LAST

Periwinkle

VINCA HERBACEA

When I was a very little girl and our family was, as usual, spending the summer on Cape Cod, I went one afternoon with my mother to call on a lady who had a large house—which I only dimly remember—and a short distance away from it a great old-fashioned flower garden.

This garden was laid out in a rectangle, with a broad grass footpath down the center and narrower ones at right angles. It was framed by a low white picket fence and it was jammed and crowded with the gayest flowers imaginable. There were tall delphiniums and white lilies, sweet peas of every hue and intensely fragrant, roses and daisies, with bright nasturtiums edging the paths. There were heaps and heaps of other flowers—in fact, it looked rather like one of those too vividly painted picture postcards which sell three for a penny. I thought it was simply gorgeous. I walked up and down the paths and around and around, and perhaps one reason the lilies seemed so tall was because I was so small myself. I touched with my fingers this blossom and that, and I sniffed and sniffed and screwed my eyes tight shut to better smell the mingled perfumes. I discovered later that we had a very pretty perennial border of our own, but I had never, in my brief span of life, definitely noticed and actually walked through a flower garden before.

When I was eighteen I visited on the island of Capri, and the first afternoon I was taken to tea at a nearby villa.

We came to a high white stucco wall and opened the solid wooden gate and found ourselves in a patio, green and cool in shadows, with antique amphorae on either side of an open arch. We went through the arch and up a long flight of stone stairs, and came out on a terrace on this higher level. It was partially roofed by a pergola, thick with grapevines, and a fig tree held its branches and huge leaves over a white marble table. There were white marble benches with carved bases, and carved white marble pillars framed the blue water far below. A few flowers bloomed in pots that were grouped near the splashing wall fountain, and there was a balustraded stone railing across one end of the terrace, for the cliff dropped abruptly down to the sea.

I had never seen anything like this before and I experienced the same excitement and delight that I had felt when I saw the old-fashioned flower bed on Cape Cod.

Since then I have seen many gardens in many countries, and I have planted and tended quite a few of my own. And no matter what the location or climate in which I have found myself, I have noticed that I am always trying, not entirely consciously, to make my garden like the one on Cape Cod and the one in Capri.

This is obviously absurd. An Italian terrace, an integral part of a hillside villa, high above the Bay of Naples, with a fig tree and a grapevined pergola and almost no flowers, and a Cape Cod flower bed a little distance away from a big frame house, confined by a white picket fence and patterned by grass paths, are as dissimilar as Hamlet and Hercules. But those two swift recognitions made such an emotional impress on me that my taste must have received two definite biases, so that when I plan and plant I am always striving to re-create my own humble interpretation of those beautiful visions.

As a matter of fact, my present garden does, indeed, incorporate some of the features of my two first loves. There is no vista of the Bay of Naples framed by carved white pillars, and there is none of the soft moisture of the Cape Cod air to sweeten the fragrance and intensify the bloom. Delphiniums and sweet peas do not take kindly to our hot summers; carved marble benches and tables would be too grand for our terrace. But we have a patio, shadowy and green, and a fig tree, and two weather-stained amphorae stand on either side of the door. We also have a small rectangular plat jammed and crammed with flowers. They are not distinguished specimen plants, just old-fashioned commonplace flowers which are obliging enough to bloom all through the spring and summer and the fall.

A solid garden wall encloses it all—grass and flowers, patio and fountains—making the outdoors an integral extension of indoors. Thus my diverse loves—one from Cape Cod and one from Capri—seem, at least to my prejudiced eye, to get along very amicably together.

There are two little girls who live next door, whose mother has a far handsomer and larger garden than mine, but when I see them peering through the gate and invite them in, they always seem overjoyed. They appear fascinated by the flowers growing in pots which are grouped around the fountain; they think the patio is a grand place to play, being like a room of the house and yet out of doors.

Sometimes I feel a trifle apprehensive lest their embryonic tastes receive a bias which is not entirely correct: lest, when they grow up and plan their own gardens, they will copy my mistakes simply because they associate them with a happy afternoon. It is quite a responsibility, and I hope through the years to refine and perfect my planting and minimize its faults, and thus do as little damage as possible to those gardens which will be planted long after I have gone.

For, although this is my last garden, it may be that for my two small neighbors it is their first. And a first garden, like a first love, is never forgotten.

And nearer to the river's trembling edge
　　There grew broad flag-flowers, purple prankt with white,
And starry river buds among the sedge,
　　And floating water-lilies, broad and bright,
Which lit the oak that overhung the hedge
　　With moonlight beams of their own watery light;
And bulrushes, and reeds of such deep green
As soothed the dazzled eye with sober sheen.

SHELLEY

WRIT IN WATER

Water Lily
NYMPHAEA

There are gardens which bloom not in carefully prepared beds of earth; not in forests or by roadsides; not in rocks or on desert sand; not high in the air as the Hanging Gardens of Babylon, or in penthouse enclosures above city streets. These are water gardens where, although the roots of water hyacinths, lotus and lilies are secure in the dark muck far below, all that is visible are the leaves and blossoms floating on the limpid surface.

Some of the most ancient and famous water gardens in the world are in China, and Marco Polo, visiting Hangchow in 1278, described its pleasure grounds in praise not unduly hampered by accuracy. He told the astonished Venetians that in this city were twelve hundred bridges, high enough for a fleet to pass under them. He wrote, "Within the city lies a lake thirty miles in circumference; about its shores are palaces of richest construction and the cloisters of silent monks. On a great island is a palace open to the public where citizens may give magnificent entertainments, with sumptuous accessories supplied by the city."

Dorothy Graham, in her *Chinese Gardens,* is a more reliable but not less worshipful recorder of the same pleasure grounds as they exist today, seven centuries later. The lake of Si, surrounded by a triple range of hills and flecked with islands, is such a garden. From it rises the willow-edged Island of the Three Pools of the Moon's Reflection and in this island are three lagoons, whose surface is a swaying field of lotus.

Above the lotus zigzags a bridge of vermilion lacquer—the Bridge of the Nine Windings. In the center of one pool, where it may be seen from all sides, is the Rock of the Nine Lions. One approaches this guarded enclosure of substance and shadow in a painted barge, or gazes down upon it from a pavilion overhanging the edge.

There are similar gardens reached by steps, or bordered by latticed walks, or accented by pavilions of dark wood. Courtyards of the palaces are built close to the wash of the margin, so they can look out upon the lotus, which in that climate reach the height of three or four feet in a tangled mass of verdure.

These are, indeed, water gardens, but it has taken twentieth-century inventiveness to create gardens which are entirely without soil. Hydroponics, which is also called aqua culture, water culture, tray culture or tank farming, is the growing of plants without earth of any kind, but directly from water to which has been added necessary nutrient solutions. The support for such plants may be provided by sand, pumice, glass wool, cinders, etc., or by wire baskets filled with excelsior. Or they may be held in place by wooden rings which fit into the top of a jar or vase.

In all cases the roots extend into the water and, when cared for according to directions, the plants are often taller, stronger and more productive than those grown in the usual manner. They are, obviously, free from soil diseases and, even more obviously, in no danger of drought, and while the method does not fulfill all the first extravagant promises, it is now a recognized procedure for aising both flowers and vegetables. It is a godsend in places where soil is poor or lacking, as was proved on some of the Pacific atolls where our soldiers—who probably would have scorned to dig or hoe in their home patches—happily raised tomatoes and cucumbers in water-filled hollows in the barren coral.

While individual plants thus raised may be handsome specimens, a tank farm with its pipes and mechanism is hardly esthetically pleasing. Horticulturists may experiment with hydroponics out of curiosity, and market gardeners use them for commercial reasons, but most people who garden for pleasure will probably be true to the familiar soil, which may have its diseases and droughts and will certainly make dirty both hands and feet and a fair amount of space in between.

Most people will continue to delight in those gardens where solid earth and moving water are combined in a picture which is permanent and yet constantly changing.

Italy is peculiarly fitted to create such pictures. The steepness of the mountains, the volume of the rushing streams, have made it possible to lay out grounds like those of the Villa d'Este. Here a series of lakelike ponds led to the grand fountains, with the tinkle of small fountains rising in crescendo to the crash of cascades falling to a massive basin. The alley of a hundred fountains was correctly named, for the mighty force of a natural torrent was so dispersed as to compose a symphony of rushing waters, while the elaborate wall fountain of the organ played madrigals and other music. Everywhere the plashing sound of water brought freshness into the heat of noonday and romance into the night.

At Frascati there was water to spare for pranks and tricks, such as inviting guests into a grotto and suddenly releasing a streaming curtain to bar them in.

When André de Nôtre drew the plans for Versailles at the command of Louis XIV, he designed a Grand Canal two hundred feet wide and a mile long, so that when the King gave a fête hundreds of Venetian gondolas could wind their way through it. The fountains, the basins, set with statuary—the cascades—all of these could be turned on by a servant scampering ahead of the royal promenade, and, when the King and his entourage had passed, could thriftily be turned off again.

Such prodigal use of water is possible only in countries of ample supply. But there are regions where the precious stuff must be skillfully handled to produce the greatest effect from the most meager amount, and this necessity has sometimes resulted in charming scenes.

In Andalusia, for instance, lakes or even pools could not be attempted, for water was too precious to lie idle on a silent expanse. However, the Moors who brought their ideas to Spain had no intention of being deprived of the cool refreshment. But they confined it in open terra cotta canals, so that it would murmur as it slipped along. Diminutive conduits led from tree to tree and shrub to shrub. The fountains were designed with greatest care not to waste their overflow, but to guide it so that it sparkled in the sun and heightened the luster of the tile before it was caught in a gutter and carried off in an open canal. Some of the basins have their outer brims fauceted to augment the effect of a limpid volume spilling over. Foundations of glazed tiles reflecting a thin film of moisture make it seem greater than it actually is. Tiled paths sprayed from tiny jets not only brighten and cool them but give them the liveliness of a flowing stream.

If the gardens of Andalusia made the most of what water was procurable, there are gardens in Japan which are built around the idea of water and yet have not a single drop of it. The Japanese are adepts in exploiting a tiny pool or a thread of rivulet, embellishing it with islands, boulders and lanterns. They go farther, and take dry rocks and put them together in such a way that they suggest a waterfall and its basin, the course of the winding stream conforming in every realistic detail.

But instead of actual water, gravel and sand are strewn to suggest it—an illusion immediately accepted by the Japanese and, once it is explained to them, with astonishing readiness by foreigners. Many a famous old garden in a temple compound creates such an effect with merely rocks and sand and perhaps a few trees and shrubs.

Sometimes the Japanese select a few small stones which are interesting in shape or color and arrange them in a shallow tray. These are kept constantly wet, not only to heighten their colors, but to induce a growth of moss which will, in Japanese symbolism, represent a mountain or a verdant island.

Obviously, confronted with such examples, none of us can sigh that our purse or our grounds are so small as to prohibit the introduction of water into our garden.

The floating gardens of Montezuma have intrigued the imagination since the days of Cortez, and as children we dreamily pictured them like the drifting fantasies in the poems of Christina Rossetti.

The paradox about these gardens is that they do not float but are firmly anchored to the bottom of Lake Xochimilco.

It is said that they got their name in Aztec times when rafts were built of twigs and branches, heaped with rich earth and then —at the command of the emperor chief—planted with flowers. Small trees appeared and gradually the roots from this vegetation reached down and steadied the raft.

Today the gardens, which are an hour and a half by auto from Mexico City, bear no resemblance to those early floating rafts. They are actually islands, some only a few feet square, some comprising acres, intersected by canals and waterways. They have been built up by layer upon layer of sediment and, although some quake like quicksand, others are firm enough to support houses.

From this rich soil flowers grow like mad. Purple and white stock cover whole islands; there are fields of scarlet poppies, sweet peas and daisies; there are acres of marigolds and miles of violets.

As if there were not enough actual flowers, these are duplicated by reflections, and white calla lilies edging an island are
mirrored back from the deep, dark water. Vegetables, too, grow
furiously—several crops a year—and these and the flowers are
carried daily to Mexico City by the winding waterways. It is these
narrow, pointed gardeners' boats, piled with their fresh flowers and
green vegetables, that seem like floating gardens as they are si-
lently poled along the waterway.

On weekdays it is very quiet, but on Sunday the old Viga
Canal is crowded with flower-decorated pleasure boats, and ma-
rimba bands crash and bang. When there are festivals and pageants, sometimes floating rafts are made for the occasion in the old
primitive fashion.

Flowers not only spring up on the island but heap themselves
over the low roofs of the houses, and reflect themselves in the
water. Water-lilies and blue water-hyacinths float in great masses
on the dark lake. The canals are kept free of obstruction from these
aquatic plants, but there are enough to carry the illusion of land
and water merging into a single sheet of color and perfume.

All of these gardens, dissimilar as they are, depend upon
both land and water for their value and their beauty. But there are
still other gardens which exist below the aqueous element, and
perhaps the most lovely description of these in the English language was written by Edmund Gosse in his book *Father and Son*.

In this touching autobiography, he tells how on the Devon
shore, bending beside his father over some shallow tidal pool in the
limestone rocks, he would see, mirrored in the dark hyaline and
framed by the sleek and shining fronds of oar-weed, the figures
and faces of a middle-aged man and a funny little boy. ". . . then
the rocks between tide and tide were submarine gardens of a beauty
that seemed often to be fabulous, and was positively delusive,
since, if we delicately lifted the weed-curtains of a windless pool,

hough we might for a moment see its sides and floor paved with living blossoms, ivory-white, rosy-red, orange and amethyst, yet all that panoply would melt away, furled into the hollow rock, if we so much as dropped a pebble in to disturb the magic dream.

"Half a century ago, in many parts of the coast of Devonshire and Cornwall, where the limestone at the water's edge is wrought into crevices and hollows, the tide-line was, like Keats' Grecian vase, 'a still unravished bride of quietness.' These cups and basins were always full, whether the tide was high or low, and the only way in which they were affected was that twice in the twenty-four hours they were replenished by cold streams from the great sea, and then twice were left brimming to be vivified by the temperate movement of the upper air. They were living flower-beds, so exquisite in their perfection, that my Father, in spite of his scientific requirements, used not seldom to pause before he began to rifle them, ejaculating that it was indeed a pity to disturb such congregated beauty. The antiquity of these rock-pools, and the infinite succession of the soft and radiant forms, sea-anemones, sea-weeds, shells, fishes, which had inhabited them, undisturbed since the creation of the world, used to occupy my Father's fancy. We burst in, he used to say, where no one had ever thought of intruding before; and if the Garden of Eden had been situated in Devonshire, Adam and Eve, stepping lightly down to bathe in the rainbow-coloured spray, would have seen the identical sights that we now saw,—the great prawns gliding like transparent launches, *anthea* waving in the twilight its thick white waxen tentacles, and the fronds of the dulse faintly streaming on the water, like huge red banners in some reverted atmosphere.

"All this is long over, and done with. The ring of living beauty drawn about our shores was a very thin and fragile one. It had existed all those centuries solely in consequence of the indifference, the blissful ignorance of man. These rock-basins, fringed by corallines, filled with still water almost as pellucid as the upper air itself, thronged with beautiful sensitive forms of life,—they exist no longer, they are all profaned, and emptied, and vulgarised. An army of 'collectors' has passed over them, and ravaged every corner of them. The fairy paradise has been violated, the exquisite product of centuries of natural selection has been crushed under the rough paw of well-meaning, idle-minded curiosity. That my Father, himself so reverent, so conservative, had by the popularity of his books acquired the direct responsibility for a calamity that he had never anticipated, became clear enough to himself before many years had passed, and cost him great chagrin. No one will see again on the shore of England what I saw in my early childhood, the submarine vision of dark rocks, speckled and starred with an infinite variety of colour, and streamed over by silken flags of royal crimson and purple."

If those submarine visions will never again be seen on the shores of England, neither is there likely to be another writer who could describe them as did Edmund Gosse.

For me, the loveliest water garden is one that is near the sea, or a lake, or a river. The liquid element, translucent, blue, or misty gray, or glossy black, gives a fourth dimension.

Celia Thaxter planted, tended, loved and wrote about her flower beds and borders on the small island of Appledore, and went to and fro, spring and fall, from the New England mainland in a boat piled high with roots and slips, and plants and baskets of bulbs. Although that was more than half a century ago, her flowers still give pleasure to those who turn the pages in which she so tenderly, so valiantly describes them.

Flowers are larger and more intense in hue in air cooled and moistened by encircling water, as you may see if you float through the archipelago of the Swedish coast, with its many hundreds of islands pricked out with the roof of a single cottage or a cluster of summer houses; as you may see from Guanabara Bay as you look up at the hillsides of Rio de Janeiro, filigreed by pergolas and terraces and winding paths, and enameled in rose and gold and green. The island of Capri is a great jewel of a garden set in the matrix of the Bay of Naples, jewel and setting changing in tone and texture with every shifting hour.

Matthew Arnold, in mournfully sublime syllables, caresses the idea that each human life is an island separated from all the other myriad millions by the unplumbed sea. But when the moon lights their hollows and they are swept by the balms of spring, then, with a longing like despair, they feel that they were once parts of a single continent. Sundering straits lie between them, and in times of grief these are bitter and salt. In times of happiness they dream of coming closer—so close that their margins meet.

Matthew Arnold did not suggest it in his famous lines, but at certain times we discover for ourselves that those islands which seemed to be bare, lonely rock reveal, as we come closer to them, that they are hidden gardens.

I once saw a botanist most tenderly replace a plant which he had inadvertently uprooted, though we were on a bleak hillside in Tibet, where no human being was likely to see the flower again.

SIR FRANCIS YOUNGHUSBAND

Though we travel the world over to find beauty, we must carry it with us or we find it not. . . .

EMERSON

TRAVELER'S GARDEN

Morning Glory

IPOMEA PURPUREA

People who love their gardens are not necessarily those who stay most closely in them. The green thumb and the wandering foot are not incompatible.

But your garden lover finds an interest in travel which the non-garden lover does not know. For every part of the globe reveals some flower or lichen, some tree or herb, some shrub or moss which catches his eye, perhaps because it is a familiar form in a totally strange place or perhaps because it is utterly unfamiliar.

The first time we see a coconut palm slanting against a tropical sky is as memorable as our first leaving the ground in an airplane. To come across a great clump of rhubarb, precisely like that in our own vegetable patch, blooming robustly far beyond the Arctic Circle, where it is too cold for even potatoes, is sharp astonishment.

Of course, your true gardener is never content merely to observe an unknown plant. He must bring home a clipping or a root or at least a few seeds to try in his own flower bed or border, an ambition he modestly shares with certain illustrious personalities.

The Empress Josephine, who was so charming that she captivated Napoleon and so frivolous that she lost him, was never more charming or less frivolous than in her role as gardener. She had traveled far from her birthplace in Martinique to the courts of Europe, and she extended these travels vicariously through those of her husband. At Malmaison, her retreat near Paris, she set out with her own hands plants which she commandeered from places which were, two hundred years ago, far away indeed in space and time. Her plunder from Napoleon's conquests included the soldanella from the Alps, the violet of Parma, the carnation of Lodi, the willow and the plane of Syria, the water-lily of the Nile, the hibiscus of Palestine, and the rose of Damietta.

With exertion and intelligence, which she rarely exercised otherwise, she studied soils and climates, rocks and sands. She experimented with grasses, shrubs and trees and ruled as a jealous despot in the flowery kingdom she created and to which, at certain times, she invited selected visitors. After her days of power and glory were over, it was to Malmaison she came to finish her life in dignity, surrounded by the flowers which had never failed her and which she, on her part, had never neglected or betrayed.

At about the same time that the Empress who had been born in the West Indies was creating Malmaison, Thomas Jefferson, who had been born in Virginia, was planning and planting his gardens at Monticello. The man who served as Governor of Virginia, Secretary of State in Washington's cabinet, Vice-President and President of the United States, and for eighteen years was president of the American Philosophical Society, and who founded and designed the University of Virginia, was one of the most indefatigable traveler-gardeners the world has ever known. Although he was forced to be away from home a greater part of the forty years he was in public service, he never forgot his gardens, and his huge garden book covers entries from 1766 to 1824, two years before his death.

In this we read of how he was continually sending home from abroad seeds and plants with instructions as to their cultivation. And he was almost as continually asking to have sent him from his own estates seeds, nuts, slips and plants which he wished to give to his friends. To him the South owes the mimosa tree (*Albizzia julibrissin* Durazzini) with its feathery-leaved branches and perfumed puffs of bloom. To correct soil erosion on hillsides, he introduced the broom whose bright, strong yellow flowers and vibrant green branches glorify miles of Virginia roadsides. He introduced the olive tree and dry rice into South Carolina and experimented with wine-making from vines sent from France. One of the chief purposes of the Lewis and Clark expedition, which he arranged, was to collect native Western plants to see if they could be cultivated in the East. The list of plants he imported and raised successfully is prodigious.

He continued the shipment of seeds and plants from abroad until the death of his friend, M. Thouis, Superintendent of Le Jardin des Plantes in Paris. At Monticello there were an experimental garden, two nurseries and a glassed-in piazza which served as a greenhouse. His written notes and the diagrams sketched with his own hand, the names of the flowers he planted and, in many instances, the position of the bed or border where they were placed, were so complete that it was possible for the Garden Club of Virginia to restore the flower beds and the walks and lawns with greatest accuracy.

From France and Italy and England he sent seeds and plants, and up to the end of his life he knew and noted every single thing which came up through the rich earth of his carefully prepared beds.

This is a traveler's garden without compare!

Few of us have the acres and plentiful assistance of Josephine and Jefferson to experiment thus. But some of us yield not one iota to either of them in curiosity and expectations which bob up, sanguine in spite of disappointments.

Once I saw, clambering and tangling over a mud hut in the Andes, morning-glories of such size and such a pure celestial blue that I had to stop and examine them more closely. The flower, except for its immensity and color, was like our common annual, but the leaf was quite different. The Indian woman came out and smiled at me and, although she spoke no English and I no Quicha, she understood immediately that I was begging a few seeds. She gave them freely and I put them in an envelope and carried them in my purse for months and, finally, the following spring, planted them in my window box at home.

They came up readily and the leaf was true to the Andean ones. Never were morning-glories so solicitously tended as those in my window box. In proper time a bud appeared—and then one morning the flower opened. It was a specimen of mean size and of a muddy magenta—quite the ugliest morning-glory I ever saw.

Of course, I have kept on trying. I have even brought a small madroña tree from British Columbia—purchased at a nursery and scientifically packed by an expert nurseryman. The madroña—also called the arbutus, for it belongs to the *Ericaceae*—is one of the most striking and lovely trees on earth. The bark of its trunk is the color of copper and bronze, and it shreds and peels away during the summer, leaving a smooth and delicate new bark beneath. Its narrow leaves are evergreen, its blossoms white and swooningly fragrant, like those of the trailing arbutus of the same family. It may grow tall and straight, but when it is buffeted by winds or manipulated by a skillful gardener it may be fantastically twisted.

I could not give it the fresh moist air from the Pacific Ocean, but I could and did give it a soil which was sharpened and lightened with disintegrated rock, and it promptly died.

That this was not the fault of the tree but entirely mine is proved by the fact that it has been successfully planted in an alien climate, for when the native sons of British Columbia sent a tree to mark the grave of Captain George Vancouver in England, they chose the arbutus. The gardeners of Kew nursed and nurtured it until it could be transplanted to the cemetery at Petersham. Here, in the empire ceremonies, it holds a place of honor when a wreath is placed upon the grave of the first white man to sail into the inner harbor of the city which bears his name.

That all transplantations are failures is, of course, disproved by looking at any garden from Maine to Florida where there bloom, quite as a matter of course, flowers which were native to quite different lands. The tuberous-rooted begonias came originally from the Andes; gladioli, iris and freesias from South Africa. Primulas are from China; rhododendrons from the Himalayas. Switzerland is the home of some of our most loved gentians, Asia of the forget-me-not (*Myosotis scorpioides*) and Turkestan of the *Tulipa kaufmaniana*.

These, and many others, have been improved and hybridized: made larger or smaller; made ruffled or doubled or tripled, and most of us have forgotten that they are not natives but grew originally in quite different soils and climates. Thus, Chinese traders carrying their silks and sandalwoods to India brought back with them, two thousand years ago, the oleander, spices, drugs, coriander and cucumber. They brought the peach from Persia and grapes and walnuts from Rome. (They used the grapes only for decorative purposes and the walnuts, aged and polished, were rolled in the hands of scholars to keep their fingers supple to manipulate their writing brushes.) One Chinese emperor, who lived a hundred and forty years before Christ, collected so many rare plants that it took thirty thousand slaves to care for them, which makes Thomas Jefferson's plantations seem rather insignificant.

The English eagerly purchased plants brought back by the

East India Company—Persian lilac, white narcissus, Asiatic magnolia, crab apple, and even laurel from Tibet. The international exchange of flowers and shrubs and trees was not channeled only by trade routes.

When the Franciscan fathers came up to California from Mexico to establish their missions, they brought with them seeds of Spanish oranges and olives and dried bundles of grapevines, and thus laid the foundation for California's agricultural greatness. Nor did they forget the Castilian rose.

It was foresightedness and thrift on the part of the Franciscans to begin such plantations for the glory of the Church, but it was an humbler and more personal impulse that moved our pioneer women, leaving the East for the Middle or Far West, packing their household necessities into the covered wagon, to slip a twist of paper with a few seeds into a drawer or between the leaves of a book. They managed somehow to plant them and somehow to tend them, so that when they were far away from the place where they had been born they could rest their eyes on flowers which reminded them of home.

Wives of missionaries bound for Hawaii did more than take a few seeds. One such devoted female carried a small lantana in a pot all the way from New England around the Horn to the island of Oahu. She got it there alive, planted it, and was rewarded by a Jack-and-the-Beanstalk phenomenon. For it grew and it grew; it opened its flowers and shook out its seeds, so that today from that one plant there are whole forests of lantana trees and they are such a pest they have to be destroyed.

The principle worked in reverse. Robert Fortune, a missionary to China in 1830, sent back to this country and helped introduce certain varieties of peaches, chrysanthemums and clematis.

The Occident received from the Orient spirea, many azaleas, forsythia, tree peonies and the kerria, which they class with the "noisy" flowers.

Not all such importations were lawfully acquired.

The Brazilian government, hoping to keep a monopoly on the Para rubber tree, which was once found only in the Amazon basin, prohibited the exportation of a single seed.

But England was not slow to see the potential value of such plantations in her own tropical colonies. First one and then another expedition was sent out from Kew Gardens to obtain *Hevea* seeds, and they were unsuccessful. Finally (1876), Kew Gardens sent out H. A. Wickham who was familiar with the lower Amazon. He investigated several localities, realizing that the seeds had to be most carefully chosen if they were to survive the long voyage to England. At last he discovered a promising area, and chartered a small sea-going steamer which came up the Amazon, and loaded it with seven thousand seeds crated in Indian baskets with dried wild banana leaves between each two layers of seeds, for, as he wrote later, he knew "how easily a seed so rich in drying oil becomes rancid or too dry, and so losing all power of germination."

With his precious freight he sailed boldly down the river and passed through customs by the simple expedient of declaring his cargo to be "exceedingly delicate botanical specimens."

He had done his work well. Nearly three thousand of the seeds germinated in Kew Gardens, and a few of the young plants were subsequently shipped, with extraordinary care and protection, to Ceylon and Singapore. Today there are millions of Hevea trees in the Far East.

Early traders, pioneer women, Franciscan friars and missionaries in general, even Thomas Jefferson and the Empress Josephine, were not professional botanists. Since their day expert scientists have been sent out with government support from many countries to study the useful and ornamental plants in various parts of the world, in order to introduce them at home.

I know few more fascinating books than David Fairchild's *The World Was My Garden,* which relates his travels and discoveries and shipment of tropical fruit trees from Africa and Java, cotton and dates from Egypt, rice from Japan and melons from western Asia. Hundreds of thousands of trees, shrubs and plants; miles of grain, immense plantations of fruits and vegetables from Nova Scotia to Florida, and from Alaska to Panama, are the beautiful and profitable result of such transplantations.

These achievements are on such a gigantic scale that it is easy to lose sight of the romance and painstaking labor which went into their accomplishment. Fairchild's book recaptures this so vividly and simply that never again can we purchase a pot of African violets or some rhizomes of Japanese iris, or order a Lombardy poplar or a Norway spruce, or visit a botanical garden or a plant experiment station without a thrill of wonder.

Instead of being discouraged by these tremendous introductions of once alien plants, we are merely spurred on in our own small ventures. When we travel we will always be tempted, and yield to the temptation, to bring home seeds and slips and experiment with them, and they will sometimes flourish and more often they will fail.

Perhaps we would be wiser if we came home with a less tangible but more important cargo of ideas. For it is almost impossible to see gardens in other parts of the world and not learn certain things which are applicable to our own situations and limitations.

Recently I visited, in Ontario, a garden of great extent and effectiveness, bordering the St. Lawrence River. It had terraces and stairways and waterfalls; it had rock gardens and cutting gardens and ornamental gardens and properly concealed greenhouses and potting sheds and all the rest. As I walked through it, I was struck by the fact that this magnificent display was based not on a great diversity of plants or even upon particularly rare ones. There were zinnias and Chinese bellflowers; there were pinks and phlox and stock and verbena—gorgeous because they stood in masses and drifts large enough to hold their own under a vast sky and beside a wide river.

Seeing these matter-of-fact and usual flowers so handsomely disposed and so meticulously tended was like going to a party in a particularly splendid house and finding there, not a crowd of strangers but congenial friends and pleasant acquaintances. They are all dressed their very best, and their faces are so gay and happy that at first we think they are wearing brand-new clothes. But this is only because they are so sprucely groomed. There may be a few strangers and maybe we will enjoy meeting them, but the party is a success not because of the guests we do not know but because of those we do. It is hard to know people—or flowers—well and not have some kind of fondness for them, although this noble sentiment may be better for the confession that there are some people—and some flowers—which are frankly tiresome and which we would be delighted never to encounter again.

Another thing that made this Ontario garden memorable was that it was not an unbroken sheet of colors. The brilliance was relieved by quiet places where there was only foliage to mark where flowers had been. The columbines had long since gone, but their lovely leaves were turning bronze. The primroses spread their little mats of green, although no bright flowers with jewels in their hair danced upon them. The chrysanthemums, just budding, were staunch and sturdy. There was room enough for those flowers which had bloomed, and those which were blooming, and those which would bloom. Therefore, the garden, in spite of its palatial features, was truly a home for flowers and not a horticultural display where every inch is filled with a specimen at the peak of its bloom, like an orchestra which plays from the beginning to the end of a performance with never a diminuendo.

While it is great fun to bring home seeds and slips and plants from our travels, just as it is fun to experiment every year with something we have never tried before, it is the part of caution to test these out in some separate spot where their failure will not spoil the over-all picture. Time enough to brag when—or if— they flourish.

Sometimes what we want is nothing exotic but like the Moors who, when they moved used to carry with them their gardens in great earthen pots ready to be placed in a new courtyard, we crave flowers which we loved when we lived in another part of the country. Delphiniums and sweet peas grow easily enough in what the garden books prosaically call zones one, two and three. But the Northerner who tries to gratify a nostalgic desire and plants them in zone five, for instance, should be braced for disappointment, as should the Southerner who hopes, in a Northern garden, to gather figs from fig trees—although, as a matter of fact, there are figs which can be nursed through the winters of New York and Minnesota.

To be sure, one cannot claim distinction when everything in her garden may be found in everyone else's, and at the same time. But neither nostalgia nor vanity is the best guide toward a happy garden. After all, our hats and hair-do—even our features— are more or less similar to those of our neighbors and contemporaries, and yet we manage to remain recognizable. With quite usual material we can create our own effects. If this procedure seems a bit tame, like that of people who do their boldest thinking along the safest lines, we can find some satisfaction in being pleasing even if we are not startling.

This does not mean that we will not often think of those faraway flowers and trees which we will never see again unless we return to the distant places where they grow.

Often I think of a treeless, swampy pasture, where ten thousand glittering round white tassels sparkle in the sun and quiver in the wind. They look like snow, only every flake is enormous, and they grow so close that they are touching one another. These are the heads of the silk grass—or wool grass or cotton grass—which grows in the boggy ground of Iceland. Airy as flecks of moonlight, they sweep for miles and miles. The Icelanders call them Fiva, and I have gathered them—my feet sucked by the marsh—and brought them home to use on occasion for a winter bouquet, for they keep perfectly for years. I believe they grow in many other places besides Iceland, but it is only there that I have seen them and been enraptured by their spectral delicacy.

Huge, short-stemmed begonias in palest yellow, in softest pink, in red and white, loll on the graves in a cemetery whose paths are sanded and raked into patterns or pressed into designs. Upon the headstone of each grave there is a star with the date of the birth, and a cross with the date of the death. This cemetery is in Finland, and although there are begonias in many gardens—even in my own—I have never seen any so lush as those which mark the graves of a stern folk who, in a country where there is no month of the year unthreatened by an iron frost, wrested bleak livelihoods from a stony soil. Now, for two months in every year, their graves are blanketed by this gentle luxuriousness.

I think of the madroña with its bark in metallic tints, with its bright leaves buffeted by the winds from the salt Pacific, and I try to recall the penetrating perfume of its white flowers.

I think of the strange dark mangrove trees, flinging their roots out into the air to curve and drop down into the dark waters of the Rio Dolce flowing into the Gulf of Honduras. The mangrove swamp is fearsome and along the edge where it meets the river, the exposed snakelike roots—as thick as the arm of a man—form a tangled thicket, interlacing and arching down into the gloomy water.

The purpose of this shudderingly grotesque formation is not to terrify the passing boatman. The roots, in advance of their parent stem, are taking possession of the mud and gradually, with strange beneficence, they will reclaim it from the water and contribute it to the land.

I cannot have these flowers and trees in Virginia. I do not know when I shall travel to see them again. But I cannot forget them and often, when it is very quiet in my garden, I find my trowel motionless in my hand as I am thinking of faraway places.

And then I close my eyes that I may clearly see.

Dost thou not see the little plants, the little birds, the ants, the spiders, the bees working together to put in order their several parts of the universe?

MARCUS AURELIUS

DURABLE FLOWERS

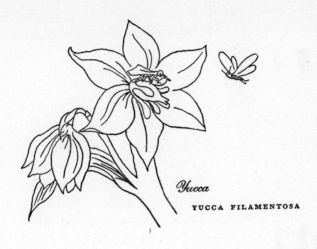

Yucca

YUCCA FILAMENTOSA

On the wall of a certain Cape Cod cottage there hung, when I was a child, a picture under glass in a dark wood oval frame. From a little distance it looked like a wreath of flowers, either painted or delicately drawn and tinted. It was only on closer inspection that its actual materials and workmanship were revealed. It was a wreath, it is true, but the stems of the flowers were fashioned of brown hair tightly wound around a twig or wire, and the blossoms, buds and leaves were of similar filaments, woven, frizzed, braided, twisted, looped or knotted.

There was, I remember, a cluster of lilies-of-the-valley, the tiny bells wrought from snow-white hair. There were black-eyed Susans, with pale yellow rays and black seedlike centers. One tiny red rosebud fascinated me especially, as the extreme fineness of the still glossy threads suggested that a lock had been clipped from the head of a brick-topped baby. Some of the russet leaves had central veins of gray. Altogether, it was an ingenious and intricate affair, representing much painstaking labor, and for me there was nothing in the least gruesome about these human gleanings. I do not suppose the woman who contrived it was seeking to create an enduring floral masterpiece so much as to preserve mementoes of the family, for grandma and grandpa, parents, children and a fairly wide assortment of relatives must have contributed toward it. At any rate, it had hung on the wall for more than a century, a memorial wreath of astonishing changelessness.

I was reminded of the Cape Cod room years later, in France, when for the first time I saw, decorating the graves in a cemetery, wreaths made of glass beads. These were obviously highly practical. Sun does not wither them, ice and snow do not crack them and rain does not stain them. They are sometimes very pretty and it is easy to see why they are popular with the thrifty French.

There was, at that period, quite a vogue for pressed ferns, flowers and grasses, mounted and framed, and occasionally today we see, in a highly modern décor, striking Japanese arrangements, such as the long stalks and seed-flecked silk of milkweed, set in panels with the glass flush with the surface of the wall.

However, these ornaments have rather given way to artificial flowers—exquisite white or pink cyclamens in appropriate pots; bowls of tulips and great sprays of dogwood, of which the stems are genuine but the flat, level blossoms are of a fabric so cleverly treated that one must actually touch them to make sure they are not real. Except in careful period rooms, it is not the present fashion to put wax flowers under glass bells, but to use and place them in such a way that they appear entirely natural, enlivening a window sill, or kindling their little fire of scarlet and orange, to be reflected in the polished top of a table.

The best of these are small masterpieces, and if one were to make any criticism it would be not of the flowers themselves but of the way they are used. For the prettiest bowl, vase or pot of artificial flowers, if left in the same place indefinitely, loses the charm peculiar to real flowers and becomes merely a stationary accent in the decorating scheme. If one were clever enough or rich enough or had storage space enough to change and alternate such arrangements frequently, they would be enjoyed with fresh pleasure. For, as Proust remarks, it is seeing things which puts them in a room and not seeing which takes them away.

The small and precious Chinese jewel trees and flowers are valued not because of their verisimilitude, but because of their exquisite use of rare materials and their skilful design and workmanship. Little rosebushes and chrysanthemums of green nephrite have flower buds and leaves of coral, pearls and amber, and the fine container or dish in which they stand is filled with red coral grains to represent earth. Some of these in our museums are hundreds of years old, without a break or flaw.

The most remarkable fadeless flowers in the world are in the Ware Collection in the Botanical Museum of Harvard University. Every proper Boston child has been taken to see what does not look like a museum but like florists' cases of living plants. However, the two hundred thousand people who visit it every year are not confined to children. It is a laboratory for taxonomists, cytologists and biologists. These glass flowers are priceless not only because of their beauty but because of their scientific accuracy. Some of the models show roots as well as the stems, leaves and blossoms; some show cross sections magnified to illustrate with amazing accuracy the processes of cross- and self-pollinization by bees, butterflies, flies and other insects.

The yellow-green lady's-slipper (*Paphiopedilum insigne*) has a bee entering its saclike lip. There are three scabiosas (*Succisa pratensis*) in three different stages of development, and to the one in flower clings a butterfly with lifted wings. A brown bee with transparent wings braces itself on a flower of Scotch broom (*Cytisus scoparius*), pressing apart the keel so that the closely coiled pistil is springing back to touch the bee's back and leave pollen upon it. The strange tropical *Aristolochia fimbriata*—

Dutchman's-pipe and Viriginia snakeroot belong to the same genus—has a flower with a tubular calyx lined with rigid hairs pointing downward and opening into a dilated portion. In a cross section we can see the flies which have found their way into this trap and are unable to escape. Several hours must pass before the calyx tube will become flaccid and the hairs wither, making it possible for the flies to get out and make their way with their load of pollen to the receptive stigma of younger flowers.

There is a pale mauve blossom of our common Adam's-needle (*Yucca filamentosa*) with a moth of the same color visiting it and effecting pollination, and also a cross section showing a moth laying her eggs in the ovary, which is the only way flowers of this species can be pollinated.

These are only a few of the one hundred and sixty-four families of flowering plants and selected groups of cryptograms illustrating complicated life-histories and a group of rosaceous fruits illustrating the effects of fungus diseases.

The collection is unique, fascinating to the layman, of greatest value to the student of natural history and probably never to be duplicated.

It is the work of two men, Leopold Blaschka and his youngest son Joseph, absolutely unaided by assistants, and devoting themselves to it exclusively for nearly fifty years. Workmanship in decorative glass was traditional in this Bohemian family which came originally from Venice. They were also naturalists who had traveled in many parts of the world. Their glass models of the marine fauna of the North Sea, the Baltic and the Mediterranean are to be found in other museums, but their several thousand glass models of plants and flowers are only in the Botanical Museum at Harvard, a memorial gift of Mrs. Elizabeth Ware and her daughter.

It is not correct to call these glass flowers durable, for they are so fragile that they are broken unless handled most delicately, but they are immune from fading and decay. They were wrought in a small room kept at a temperature of 85-95 degrees, with the Blaschkas wearing masks lest their breath disturb the glass. Their tools were a Bunsen burner and tweezers. Part of the color was fused in the glass, part of it added while it cooled and part of it applied afterward. So scrupulous were the artist-craftsmen that they once made twenty models of some peach blossoms before they achieved the perfect shade and texture which met their exacting standards.

Here at last they are arranged; bouquets of mignonette and forget-me-nots; a branch of pale pink apple blossoms; a cluster of rhododendron encircled by its glossy leaves; a stalk of goldenrod thirty inches long—safe from the breakage of custom house clearances and protected from any vibration which might shatter their exquisitely wrought filaments.

Beautiful as these glass flowers are, their purpose is primarily scientific. Even if an individual could purchase them they would not be suitable as casual decoration in a private house.

Most of us must fall back on winter bouquets, leaves and grasses to brighten our rooms when the ground outside is covered with snow and ice. Everlastings, Chinese lantern, heather, thrift, polygonum, honesty—these will hold their cheerful grace until the budding boughs of winter jasmine and forsythia can be cut and brought into the house for early flowering.

Cacti are not merely durable but well-nigh indestructible if one has the heart to keep them parched for weeks and then soak them thoroughly. In those Northern countries where the winter is so long that every verdant thing is cherished, cactus plants are sometimes kept and handed down for generations, and remain staunch under conditions which would discourage anything else.

However, dried flowers, artificial flowers, sprays of evergreen, the trailing leaves of wandering Jew and philodendron, do not entirely satisfy the gardener who, even when there are more flowers than can be conveniently cut and handled, still wants to prolong the life span of his favorites.

It is natural to want the flowers we have planted and tended, and whose blooming we have so eagerly anticipated, to hold their perfection as long as possible, whether they are left to complete the garden picture or are cut for the house. The very existence of a plant may depend upon the longevity of its flowers, for if space is limited one cannot afford to give a dozen peony plants the room they require, since they contribute their beautiful balls of bloom for only a week or so, and if they are beaten by untimely showers, may be shattered almost immediately. Conversely, certain snobbish folk scorn the petunia because of its continuous and indiscriminate generosity.

Horticulturists are constantly working to extend the flowering season by developing strains of tulips, lilies, iris and chrysanthemums which bloom successively—early, midseason and late.

Neither is there lack of instruction on how to treat cut flowers. We are told to bruise, bang, crush and slash woody stems, and to singe certain succulent ones over a flame or thrust them into boiling water. For bamboos, or any reeds with hollow stems, notches cut in the upper part of each internode of the three joints which are immersed will permit the water to flow in and fill each joint. Of course, all cut flowers are to be kept out of drafts, and in a temperature as cool and moist as possible. The more indolent of us are offered powders and pellets to dissolve in the water of vases to extend the freshness of flower arrangements.

Newer and swifter methods of transportation are bent toward the same end of prolonging the life of flowers. Refrigerated holds in ships, refrigerated cars on trains and refrigerated storage space on planes are not sentimental but financially profitable ventures. At a recent chrysanthemum exhibition in Seattle, Washington, flowers were flown from Denmark and arrived in perfect condition. This is a far cry, indeed, from the year 281 when fleets laden with roses ailed from Alexandria and Carthage to the Emperor Carinus in Rome, and caravans from Milan were dispatched with the same freight to the same potentate.

Recently, a new invention was put on the market. All you have to do is to buy a certain chemical which, according to the advertisements, when sprayed over freshly cut flowers, covers them with a filmlike coat which "preserves them in all their original colors for months."

What an invention this is! Now we can pick jonquils in April, "set" and spray them, and they last until July. We can make magnificent arrangements of ruffled white petunias which will last until September. One vaseful of brilliant zinnias will hold the fort until the chrysanthemums take over, and these will last until the time for apple blossoms. Four arrangements a year, instead of three or four a week, will certainly take care of the whole business nicely.

We can reduce our cutting garden to a few square feet and reduce the endless hours spent in picking, arranging, selecting and washing containers, and discarding the imperative succession of floral visitors.

I am intrigued by this invention, and I would certainly give it a trial if I lived in an apartment and had to buy every tulip and iris and nurse it through city heat and dust.

It might seem hardly necessary to make such heroic efforts to preserve our summer flowers, for they spring into abundant life even in the most far-flung and unlikely places. On the slopes of mountains around Magdalena Bay, within a few hundred miles of the North Pole, there are in midsummer sweeping stretches of red saxifrages, and masses of heathlike *Andromeda tetragon* with drooping waxen blooms. One can walk over green and golden moss, and rest upon rocks furred with black lichens and gather Arctic buttercups and poppies. In this longitude there are even trees—polar willows are everywhere. To be sure, they reach the

height of barely two inches, and only their tips are visible over th
moss. But they are trees, nevertheless, complete with trunks an
branches, and are honored by the name *Salix polaris*.

On the very edge of the Arctic Ocean in Petsamo, you ca
pick in midsummer armfuls of golden trollius and blue anemones

However, there are certain northern reaches where there ar
no trees—not even two-inch ones—and no flowers, only the
silvery Iceland moss. It is, logically, called reindeer moss, since the
Lapland reindeer paw away the winter snow to nibble its powdery
stems and leaves.

Yet even here the passion for colorful vegetation combats the
inclemencies of climate, as I was reminded one summer in northern Finland.

The monotonous, bleak scene was stretching endlessly to the
horizon on every side when, as our car neared a remote telegraph
station, there flashed forth a great circular bed set out in symmetrical
pattern and brilliantly and variously hued. I had, of course, to stop
the car and run over to it, kneel down and examine what manner
of flowers could bloom in such profusion in that chill and windswept waste. The matlike, wiry plants were low and close-set: the
crimsons and purples, the gold and white, the blues and lavenders
contrasting and intermingling. I sought out the solitary telegraph
operator. What plants were these, I inquired in faltering Finnish?
He shrugged his shoulders a bit shamefacedly, although I was the
one who should have been ashamed, since his English was perfect.
It was, he explained, merely a patch of the ubiquitous Icelandic
moss which, with the aid of a blowgun and many pots of paint,
he had colored to suit his fancy. So that was how HE made his
garden last.

Icelandic moss should, perhaps, not be called durable but
eternal.

Cladonia lichen—*Cladonia rangiferina* is its botanical name
—is one of those pioneer plants which came in the wake of the ice

ge to lay the foundation for soil. Whoever wants to know more
bout lichens can find their story in *This Flowering World,* by
Rutherford Platt, and after reading those pages will hereafter regard this humble growth with immense respect.

Lichens endure in the most violent fluctuations of temperature; in dryness, in moisture, on stone, on wood; they cling to the
marble columns of ruined Greek temples; to boulders in New
England pastures; to fence posts, to buildings and to dry bare
pastures; they creep over disintegrating lava fields in arctic regions,
flushing those otherwise sterile stretches with glowing muted
tones. In torrid or subzero zones lichens find a hold. Only the
impure air of cities defeats them.

Some are so flat that they seem merely stains on a rock. Some
flap like curled patches of old shoe leather. Some—like the British
soldier lichen—stand erect, an inch tall, with a red cap. Some suggest miniature shrubs or trees. They are bright yellow, white,
chocolate brown, silver, black.

The lichen not only exists in the most extraordinarily diverse
regions and shapes, but it is formed in the most extraordinary way,
for it is created by the union of a fungus and an alga and looks
and acts like neither of them.

The two plants of a lichen can be seen through a microscope,
the thread of the fungus compactly massed around the green cells
of the alga. If separated, the lichen will cease to exist, although the
alga will continue its algal life and the fungus its fungal one. But
their life spans are not to be compared with the longevity of the
time-defying perennial which together they have formed.

Most lichens are so small that they seem negligible. As a
matter of fact, they are fundamental to the earth. Where the wind
has sprinkled a puff of dust on an ice cap a lichen sets its threads.
On a windswept Alpine slope it steadfastly clings.

It seems incredible that its soft and infinitesimal threads can
penetrate a rock which a steel needle, even under terrific hammer

blows, cannot dent. Here, again, it reveals another extraordinar
ability. It brews an acid so powerful that it can, in time, dissolv
the hardest crystal in granite. When it has thus etched the rock,
thrusts its thread into the opening. These acids—more than on
hundred and forty have been discovered by chemists—give the sal
crystals their sparkling oranges, reds, yellows and silvers. After th
lichen has etched the rock, humus collects in the crevice. A see
lodges in it, spores fall on it, and gradually there appear moss
ferns, grass, even harebells and saxifrages—even a birch. Thu
lichens, which require no nourishment from the soil, but get thei
sustenance entirely from the air, perfect the chemistry of the soi
for the roots of trees and flowers.

When we speak of durable plants, we must certainly begin
with the lichen, although comparatively few gardeners consider the
patch of green on a stone as a plant, and it does not encourage too
constant observation since it is the slowest growing plant in creation. We might watch a plant an inch across for many years and
see no perceptible increase.

Glass flowers, dried flowers, exquisitely fashioned flowers of
wax; jewel trees, floral arrangements "set" and preserved by
magical mist; the French funeral wreaths of colored beads; the old
hair wreath in the Cape Cod cottage—these all endeavor to preserve the loveliness of flowers. In some instances they are achievements of genuine artistic merit.

There is only one fault common to them all. They are static.
Living flowers are evanescent.

From bud to blossom to full-blown glory, they rise erect toward the sky. In their gentle decline, they droop toward the soil
which will soon cover them. Their birth and dissolution conform
in their minutest fluctuation to cosmic law. Their ephemeral gar-
ments are from earth. Their eternal cycle is part of the pattern
which embraces the heavens and the planets and the stars and all

hat lies beyond them. Beauty is their outward virtue. Obedience
o law is their inner grace.

There are many ways by which human beings preserve the
features of those they loved. How old is the mummy of that
Egyptian queen who lies in her still-bright cerements, with her
favorite cat, forever motionless, held in her arms? Her body is
here, quite perfect. But the sound of her voice, the touch of her
hand, her smile and her tears are vanished.

So it is with flowers. The tiny pulse which is their life slows
down and ceases. Their scented breath cannot be caught on any
mirror. But in the spring they will rise again and laugh through
the eyes of a thousand plants.

We do not reject those durable flowers which hold their form
and hue changeless and unfading through the months and even
through the years. We stand before them in astonishment and
often in admiration.

But when the first snowdrop and the first violet appear, we
kneel to greet them with a marveling which never grows less, although the times we have done it have grown more. We welcome
each newcomer in the pageants of spring and summer and fall, delighting in its freshness, rejoicing in its familiar form. If we were
as in tune with the infinite as they, we would, when the time
comes, be as ready to release their companionship as we were to
receive it.

"But the very reason why
I clasp them is because they die."

'Tis in ourselves, that we are thus or thus. Our bodies are our gardens; to which our wills are gardeners; so that if we will plant nettles, or sow lettuce; set hyssop, and weed up thyme; supply it with one gender of herbs, or distract it with many; either to have it sterile with idleness, or manured with industry; why, the power and corrigible authority of this lies in our wills.

—SHAKESPEARE

ANTIQUES AND HORRIBLES

Lady's-Slipper
CYPRIPEDIUM ACAULE

A generation or two ago, before there were radios and movies to entertain people, and before automobiles carried holiday-makers any distance and back again in a twinkling, people who lived in villages far away from cities found ways to entertain themselves. And one curious celebration of the Fourth of July was the procession of Antiques and Horribles.

When I was small and we spent our summers on Cape Cod, there was such a village, and every Fourth of July there was such a procession, and I waited all morning for it, although it took only a few moments for the straggling file to pass our house. However, you could see it when it appeared over the top of the hill, so you had a chance to relish the grotesque crocodile trickle to its last unsavory drop.

It was, as I remember, chiefly men and boys who disguised

themselves in rags and masks or red-painted noses or black-painted eyes, in battered hats and mismated shoes, with canes and crutches and on stilts. The object was to make themselves as frightening or as funny as possible, and the one who achieved this most horribly was awarded a prize.

I do not know if they really frightened anyone, but I do know that once I recognized a boy who had got himself up in a high hat with colored streamers, and I was very much disappointed because he looked much handsomer and more romantic than I had ever seen him. I was similarly critical of an old man with a tall staff and long white hair who, instead of being comic, had acquired a Learlike majesty. These effects were not the ones sought or admired, and such mischances never, never won a prize.

While enjoyment of the ugly or the grotesque is common enough and is the basis of much slapstick humor, we do not usually associate it with flowers. It took Des Esseintes, Huysman's symbol of decadence, to make a cult of it. This unpleasant young man ordered floral monstrosities brought to him from all over the world, and the more revolting their forms and colors the greater his morbid exaltation. He gloated over the Aurora Borealis, with leaves the color of raw meat streaked with purple. The Echinopses, swelling out from padded compresses, displayed flowers like inflamed stumps. The white leaves of a certain caladium seemed to be cut from the diaphanous bladder of a pig. Others enthralled him because they were the deep red hue of scars that have just closed or were covered with black mercurial hog lard. He never wearied of turning in his hands the pot which held a tropical pitcher-plant, for from the tip of each dark, long leaf there hung a green string—an umbilical cord—supporting a greenish urn, whose interior was covered with hair.

However, his most intense rapture came from the *Cypripedium*. This looked to him like a human tongue with taut filaments in a book on the diseases of the throat and mouth. The two little ide pieces of a red jujube color which might have been borrowed from a child's toy mill, completed the under side of the tongue, the color of slate and wine lees, and of a glossy pocket from whose lining oozed a viscous glue. (Salvador Dali might be paged at this point.) He traced the embodiment of loathsome diseases in long dark stems, seamed with gashes, in tumefied leaves abscessing blue wine and blood; in fleshy stalks showing ringlets like a pig's tail.

One can hardly read the chapter without shuddering, and, indeed, just as the plants were assembled to satisfy the perversion of Des Esseintes, so they are described to make our flesh creep.

But if, with reluctance, we should return to the pages and re-read them, we would discover that the vileness was not in the plants but in the polluted imagination of Des Esseintes. Where a rational person would see the white petals of a rose, he sees the transparent membrane which enfolds lungs suffering for oxygen. Where we would see a tree fern, he sees in the *Cibotium spectabile* a crazy structure with an enormous orang-utang tail darting through its palmated foliage—a dark hairy tail with the end twisted into a bishop's cross. On the *Cattleya* he is repelled by the design of faded lilac, an almost dead mauve, and at its scent he recoils. For the odor reminds him of toy boxes of painted pine and recalls the horrors of a New Year's Day.

Obviously, Des Esseintes was a masochist. Any normal person could placidly arrange his whole collection on a window sill and find it handsome. Those *Cypripedia* which Huysman's hero saw as a plague-tainted tongue were, after all, merely our familiar pink lady's-slippers.

There are, however, some plants which may be abhorrent to us, not because of their form, color or odor, but because of their way of getting food.

These are the carnivorous plants which, in addition to the food supplied by mother earth, and by rain and sunshine from heaven, supplement their diet by luring insects and even small vertebrates, which they digest before our very eyes.

There are a surprising number of carnivorous plants, and they have various ways of attracting, capturing and assimilating their prey, and while none of these procedures is appetizing to a human spectator, the cunningly devised mechanisms are fascinating—so fascinating that Darwin wrote a whole book about them.

The inconspicuous little butterwort or bog violet (*Pinguicula vulgaris*) has a comparatively simple method. The leaves, which are covered with hairs, are on such short stems that when fully grown they lie upon the ground. Two kinds of glands in them secrete a sticky fluid, which their margins curve inward to hold. When the insects are caught, as flies are caught on fly paper, the leaves roll over and hold them until they are digested. The sundew (*Drosera rotundifolia*) gets its name from a secretion which glistens like minute dewdrops at the tip of the many tentacles of the leaves. If anything touches these tentacles they bend over, and if this tiny tempest in a teapot was caused by an insect, he is swiftly enclosed and held until digested.

These are inconspicuous herbs, but pitcher-plants, which are carnivorous on a much more hearty scale, are often highly decorative. As their name implies, they have leaves which resemble pitchers and hold liquid in which insects, and even small animals, seeking food, are drowned.

Our common pitcher-plant, which is also called sidesaddle-flower, huntsman's-cup and Indian pitcher (*Sarracenia purpurea*) grows in marshes from Hudson Bay to Florida. The inner surface of its pitchers is lined with scalelike cells, filmed with a sweet juice. Insects, seeking the nectar, find it easy to enter the tempting bowl and impossible, because of the slipperiness of its sides, to get out of it.

One can fancy that their diet of animal life endows carnivorous plants with animal shrewdness.

Darlingtonia californica, which grows in the California uplands, has a purplish-red lamina, of fish-tail shape, hanging like a sign board at the entrance to each of its long narrow receptacles. Insects are attracted by this from considerable distances, and when they crawl inside the restaurant so temptingly advertised, find that instead of eating they are eaten. Another species has transparent spots just above the well of the leaf. These serve as windows, encouraging the insects to linger in their light, and by such dalliance increasing their chances of falling into the well.

Our northern pitcher-plants may grow from six inches to two feet, but the tropical ones (*Nepenthaceae*) are often gigantic. From a tendril-like prolongation of the midrib of each leaf hangs a curious jug, with a leaflike flap over the mouth, like a lid. They are brilliantly colored and fragrant, providing added attractions to insects and birds. Among the thirty species of *Nepenthes* is one in the mountains of Borneo with a pitcher a foot and a half long, holding enough liquid to drown a small animal or a bird. There is another in this same region which grows as an airplant on the larger branches of trees. From it hang ten-inch bags, the mouth of each a rich orange color to attract insects. Still another species, which clings to trees, has narrow urns twenty inches long, and a stalk which may be twenty feet. Sometimes the mouths of the urns are fringed with rigid points slanting inward, effectively directing traffic in a one-way route, and to a deadly destination.

Besides the plants which catch insects on their sticky hairs and hold them until they are digested, and those which, by their color and fragrance, lure not only insects but even vertebrates into their pitchers and drown them, there is a third group of carnivorous plants even more spectacular. This is Venus's-flytrap (*Dionaea muscipula*) and we do not have to journey to Borneo to see it, for it is a native of the eastern part of North Carolina.

The leaf is two-lobed, hinged and valvelike. On the margin are sharp teeth or spines, and the inner surface has three hairs on

each side. These hairs are extremely sensitive, and the instant the
are touched they act like triggers, closing the lobes tight and lock
ing the spines together. When an insect alights upon such a leaf
closes swiftly and forcibly. The victim is held fast by the sti
spines while being crushed. The leaf stays closed and becomes
stomach, and not until it has liquefied all the soft parts of th
plat du jour does it open for the next course.

There is a fourth plant, somewhat different in its mechanism
from any of the others—the bladderwort (*Utricularia*), commonl
found submerged in quiet pools and sometimes grown as a curiosit
in aquaria. There are two or three translucent green bladders o
every leaf, each with a valve which is extremely elastic and whicl
opens only inward. When a small animal pushes through thi
easily opened valve it closes instantly and cannot be opened by
pressure from within. While most of the bladderworts entrap
minute crustacea, there is one which can handle young fish and
spawn. It is even possible to photograph such a victim, its two dark
eyes showing through the wall of the bladder.

Besides these actual carnivorous plants, there are any number
of fabulous ones, such as man-eating trees which fling out their
branches octopus fashion, seizing and sucking in human beings.
There are tales of primitive religious ceremonials in which a beautiful young girl is offered as a sacrifice to such a tree. As she is
forced toward it, its green branches writhe and reach and the
thorns with which they are set come together with the force of a
hydraulic press—and thus the devil is appeased. There are rumors
of death flowers large enough for a man to walk inside, as into a
radiantly hued tent. The overpowering fragrance lulls him to sleep
and the flower, first distilling a burning acid from its calyx, closes
over him. There are flesh-eating vines and snake trees and monkey-
trap trees. Pseudo-scientists, credulous missionaries, Sunday supplement writers and travelers whose itineraries do not bear too close
verification, used to bring back such accounts. Like the dragons

nd werewolves of medieval zoology, and like giant serpents which occasionally appear on the front page of the morning paper when here is a dearth of news, these vegetable monsters are always seen n faraway places. Once they were credited to Central America, out as that part of the world has become accessible they have shifted to Madagascar and Mozambique. With the coming of the airplane to scrutinize the surface of the globe, they will be hard put to it to find a habitat.

Such carnivorous plants as are grown as curiosities in botanic gardens and greenhouses will have to do, and if we really must possess a plant which absorbs raw meat, we can buy a darlingtonia.

One does not have to be a Des Esseintes to be fascinated by the grotesque. Monstrosities in side shows rarely lack spectators and, while most people instinctively avert their eyes at the sight of an abhorrent deformity, a good many manage to take a peek.

If it seems paradoxical that flowers should be repulsive, we can remember that beauty is in the eye of the beholder. The gallon bag of the *Nepenthes rajah,* with its gaping orange mouth, is as irresistible to birds as the golden door of a saloon to a drunkard. In both cases the drink vanquishes the drinker.

The attraction of ugliness, which was the idea of the rustic procession of Antiques and Horribles of my childhood, is sometimes merely a wry sense of humor, as when a neighbor of mine decided to play a little joke on her Garden Club at its annual flower show. She went out to her border and took pains to collect magenta petunias and zinnias of poisonous yellow. She picked screamingly blue lobelia and screamingly red salvia and a wizened dahlia the color of parboiled liver. When her assortment ran out, she culled from her neighbors' gardens and finally succeeded in massing a tight solid brickbat of blossoms without one touch of greenery. Hunting farther—for this was to be a good joke—she found a tin can, washed off the label, and into this she crammed her leafless round bouquet.

Before she started for the show she gave a final look at her prospective entry and was nonplused to see that she had produced a stunningly modernistic arrangement—not at all funny and not hideous at all, but strikingly stylistic in its tubular container.

She regarded this miscarriage of her intention with disappointment. "After all," she sighed, "it's hard to make flowers look ugly."

When she told me about it I suddenly remembered the country boy with streamers in his tall hat who marched by our house one Fourth of July. He had done his best to look antique and horrible and had only succeeded in looking oddly romantic. Sometimes it is as hard to make youth look ugly as it is a bouquet of flowers.

. . . Strength may wield the pond'rous spade,
May turn the clod, and wheel the compost home;
But elegance, chief grace the garden shows,
And most attractive, is the fair result
Of thought, the creature of a polish'd mind.
—From "The Task."

WILLIAM COWPER

TWO WATERING-POTS

Columbine
AGUILEGIA VULGARIS

A number of years ago a friend sent me a watering-pot.

It is an enormous one, hand-made of pewter. It came from France and I have used it constantly for a dozen years and it is not only of especial handiness on account of its size, but it is so handsome that it is a decoration on the terrace or in the patio. When ours is not being wielded by my good right arm it stands on the rim of our dipping pool.

The other day I was working at some distance from the pool and, needing a watering-pot, seized the galvanized tin one which hangs in the garage. It is not as large as my old pewter one and, therefore, I was surprised when, after filling it with water, I found I could hardly lift it. Before I had lugged it to the appointed place my fingers were indented to the bone by the sharp narrow handle, I thought my arm must have been pulled several inches beyond its normal length and I was sure my back was broken in two places.

The answer, of course, is simple. The pewter pot is not only lighter in weight, but it is so designed—with a large rounded hollow handle which curves from the base of the spout over the top to the middle of the back—that it is perfectly balanced. The handle doesn't cut one's hand. The weight does not pull on either arm or back. And yet it holds half a gallon more water than the other.

Briefly, the beautiful French pot of classic line is more functional than the ugly new one, which looks as if it were highly utilitarian.

Everything to do with a garden should have its appropriate beauty. Why struggle with a cumbersome black rubber hose when there are plastic ones which are not injured by the sun, do not rot in the rain, are incredibly light to handle and decorative as loops of silver ribbon?

Why buy a handsome lantern for the front gate and stick near it a crudely lettered tin mail box atop a lurching post, precisely like those in squalid huddles by a rural crossroad?

Why arrange opalescent shells and stones of curious markings in cabinets in the living room when, if strewn on the bottom of the dipping pool, they would glint freshly through the water?

Why let labels and markers attached to carefully selected shrubs flap in the breeze? Why tie madonna lilies to battered stakes which have obviously been salvaged from old mops and brooms? Why let a broken peach basket filled with litter stand—even temporarily—by the roses, when the price of one of the bushes would purchase several strong and lovely baskets? Why design a back yard with no possible place to conceal the necessary trash cans?

If such details were considered, I thought, distastefully observing my own mop handles, broken peach baskets and trash cans, a garden—even a back yard—would always be pretty. It would need no extraneous ornament any more than a completely harmoniously furnished room needs irrelevant bric-a-brac.

I sat down on an iron garden chair embossed with bunches of

grapes, and wondered how I could ever have paid dollars and dollars for something too heavy to move into the breeze and which, unless scrubbed daily, smuts light-colored summer clothes and impresses upon the suffering flesh beneath the clothes an intaglio of other bunches of grapes, to say nothing of ridges and whorls.

Ponderous wooden furniture which takes two strong men to shift is no better. It is supposed to be practical, but the paint peels off it, and a wind which really means business can pitch it endwise. Bamboo and wicker chairs and settees, with circular bases which do not gouge holes in the lawn, are portable, comfortable to sit in and charming to look at, and some metal pieces are easy to handle and can be left out in the rain.

My ruminations veered to garden clothes, and I decided that they have come—or gone—a long way since the time when any old thing was the accepted attire. Today there are picturesque smocks with plenty of room for stretching and bending, and overalls, modest if not modish, which protect one's legs from insects, briers and dirt. There are gay shorts and shorter play suits, depending upon whether one prefers to be numbered among the naked or the dressed.

Such preferences, I decided, have their logical derivation from climate. In far northern countries, with long dark winters and short hot summers, people can hardly get enough of the blessed sun, and they peel their clothes down to a minimum and sprawl like flattened starfish on grass or rocks or housetops.

It may be the same desire which impels city dwellers who have only a fortnight's holiday to make tan while the sun shines. This determination to bring back to the city a testimony of an outing in the mountains or at the shore may be noted by future historians of fashionable mores somewhat as follows:

"The cult of white women to singe themselves brown was a singular characteristic of the middle twentieth century. It was not uncommon to see respectable women, even those no longer young, gathered on public beaches or beside swimming pools at summer resorts, practically naked, in full view not only of their own sex but of the opposite one, greasing and oiling themselves with a thoroughness that suggested preparing a turkey for the oven. Thus anointed, they lay in the sun in attitudes revealing their bare stomachs, thighs and middle-aged legs and feet. After their skins had absorbed as much grease as possible, they went bathing. When this occurred in swimming pools, the scum on the surface of the water, and the slime which accumulated on the sides and bottom of the pool and clogged the drains, caused much expense to the proprietors of the resorts."

After I had polished off this aspect of sun bathing, I remembered that people who live in the tropics instinctively protect themselves from the burning rays, knowing the difficulties of getting rid of a mulatto shade in a land of perpetual summer. On islands such as those in the Caribbean, where the colored race is in the overwhelming majority, ladies with Caucasian skins go to great lengths to preserve them. Aristocrats in Central and South America, proud of their Spanish heritage, prefer Castilian ivory to African ebony.

Some such medley of reflections anent garden furnishings, tools, decorations and clothing, passed through my mind as I sat nursing my bruised fingers and massaging my aching arm after my bout with the garage watering-pot.

I looked now at the staunch old pewter one, capacious, feather-light, and pleasing in its fluid lines, and realized that if the one of galvanized tin should be painted gaily, whimsically or stylishly, it would nevertheless always be awkward and hideous. Yet so accustomed do we become to the commonplace that we either resign ourselves to it, or, worse yet, cease to even see it. We plant spots of beauty in our gardens and permit details to ruin the completed picture.

I got up from the uncomfortable iron chair which was permanently grounded as far as my muscular powers were concerned and was now a red-hot griddle.

I went over to remove nursery tags from some newly planted shrubs and affixed them where they were no longer visible. I would have pulled out the mop and broom handles which were supporting the lilies, but remembered I had no inconspicuous substitutes.

I took care not to look at the trash cans in the corner of the drive near the street, awaiting the trash collector. I could build a neat walled enclosure for them for less than it would cost to make a niche for a recently acquired statue of St. Francis, whose emaciation suggested that it was he rather than the birds who was in need of nourishment.

My inclination is to build the niche first and the garbage enclosure sometime—if ever. But when the time comes to decide whether to add an embellishment or remedy an unsightly necessity, I shall thoughtfully reconsider the two watering-pots.

How well the skilful gard'ner drew
Of flowers and herbs this dial new!
Where, from above, the milder sun
Does through a fragrant zodiac run:
And, as it works, th' industrious bee
Computes its time as well as we.
How could such sweet and wholesome hours
Be reckon'd, but with herbs and flowers!

ANDREW MARVELL

CLOCK GARDEN

Dandelion

TARAXACUM OFFICINALE

It is always fascinating to observe those flowers which open in the daytime and close at night and vice versa. In Switzerland the country people call the dandelion shepherd's clock because it opens at five in the morning and closes at eight at night. Some flowers obligingly combine the offices of a barometer with those of the clock, such as the red pimpernel, which is so sensitive to atmospheric changes that it shuts its petals at the approach of rain, and has thereby gained the name of poor man's-weatherglass.

Linnaeus, after his usual scrupulous study, enumerates forty-six flowers which have similar characteristics, and lists them in three classes. First, the meteoric, which are affected by the atmosphere. Next, the tropical, because they open and close earlier and later as the length of the day increases or decreases; and lastly, the equinoctial, which open and close at a regular time.

He deals at length with the "sleep" (*somnus*) and the "wake" (*virgiliae*) of flowers, and in his *Somnus plantarum* he describes how at night certain plants fold their leaves around the tender shoots and flowers to protect them from the cold.

He seems to have been captivated by the idea at a very early age, for when he was only fifteen he made a list for a *Horologium plantarum* from which the time of day could be read by watching the opening and closing of the flowers.

He did not use this subject, as he then intended, for his doctor's thesis, but he did later devise the actual clock. This consisted of a large half circle of plants arranged around his writing table. These were selected so that each one opening at its appointed time indicated the hour of the day. While this timepiece might not be strictly accurate, for dull mornings and dry days certainly produce different responses than bright mornings and damp days, it gave much pleasure to the great botanist and was preserved for many years to give pleasure to visitors to Upsala.

To measure and record the passage of time has engaged man's attention from the dawn of civilization until this day. In Quirigua in Guatemala there stand in the jungle soil, so soft that it sinks and slides beneath the pressure of a human foot, stelae erected by the Mayas fifteen hundred years ago. Their hieroglyphics record the ordered movement of sun and moon and certain planets and compute cycles throughout three thousand centuries.

This was, indeed, an ambitious project, but plants have been often used since then to mark the course of time's wingèd chariot as it approaches and passes.

Whoever has visited Edinburgh has looked down on the sloping gardens of West Princes Street and admired the ingenious and brilliant floral clock. It is a circular garden and in the center are the two large hands, of hollow metal which is concealed by closely set plants. The hands move, by hours and minutes, pointing to the face of the clock with its twelve Roman numerals framed by a wide border whose design is changed annually to commemorate some current event.

In 1902, to honor the coronation of King Edward VII, the garden was planted in the shape of a crown, and the following year it was laid out as a clock. At first it had only one hand, to mark the hours, but later a minute hand was added. Although the numerals remain the same, the encircling frame has been variously planted, as in 1947, when the design included the coat-of-arms of the International Festival of Music and Drama and the scroll at the top included the names of Liszt and Brahms, Verdi and Grieg. It takes three men three weeks to plant the fourteen thousand plants which compose the completed design, and during the season the full time of one man to trim, weed and water the verdant timepiece.

A great variety of dwarf foliage plants is used, such as *Oxalis, Pyrethrum, Echeveria, Sedum, Thyme,* etc., in gray, green, red and cream, which are contrasted with the Waverly Blue lobelia. The designs are first sketched, submitted and passed on by the Superintendent of Parks and then enlarged on strong cardboard and cut out. This stencil is placed in position on the ground, traced and filled with the selected plants.

There are always visitors admiring and photographing this famous floral clock and speculating what event may be honored in the border the following year, and of the Americans among them surprisingly few know that they have one of their own in Cypress Lawn Memorial Park in San Francisco.

This latter is a dial rather than a clock, for although it follows the same pattern of Roman numerals planted in low-growing *Santolina,* it has no hands. The gnomon is a cypress tree covered with growing ivy and kept closely trimmed, and so placed that its shadow falls with meticulous exactness on the proper numerals. The exquisitely kept fields and interwoven borders are planted with fibrous begonias (*Luminosa compacta*), *Amaranthus, Iresine* and yellow *Pyrethrum* (carpet-of-gold).

True to California tradition, this floral dial is prodigious in size. It is fifty feet in diameter compared to the not quite twelve feet of the Edinburgh clock.

There used to be floral clocks of various types in many of the public gardens on the Continent—notably in Germany—but it was in England during the sixteenth and seventeenth centuries that the idea developed into a great number of elaborate conceits.

Logan's "Views of Cambridge" shows a dial in the gardens of Peterhouse College in 1675. A large circle was planted with box edgings cut into the proper numerals, with a clipped yew in the center for a gnomon. There was a similar one in the garden of Wentworth Castle near Barnsley.

There were also floral clocks, designed in a circle, divided into segments, like pieces in a pie, each one planted with flowers which, like the circle of plants around Linnaeus' writing table, were supposed to bloom at specified and successive hours.

Clock gardens were akin to knot gardens—those curious and elaborate plantings which originated in Holland and became part of the pretentious landscape architecture of Elizabethan England.

At this time the correct design for the great estates was to have grass only in the orchard, the bowling greens, the "wilderness" or park. The garden proper was a great square, surrounded by wide, covered walks, with similar walks dividing the central square into four or more compartments. These were marked out in a complication of "knots," which meant beds arranged in quaint patterns laid out with rule and compass in mathematical precision. Just as each compartment was filled in with "knots," so each knot was solidly planted with flowers. There was, as has been said, no grass—only the beds and the paths which divided them.

Although the designs were usually strictly geometrical, they were sometimes worked out with heraldic animals, the coat-of-arms of the owner or the date of the building of the house.

Most of the knots were raised above the level of the paths, the edges kept in place by borders of lead or tiles, wood, or even bleached sheep bones.

Old garden books are filled with designs for these knots, showing how to fill the beds inside their thick margins with a great variety of plants, so that the enclosure should suggest a mosaic of glorious contrasting or harmonizing colors. For such effects it was necessary for the plants to stand as close as possible. These were nearly all perennials, with a few hardy annuals, and it was not the individual specimen but the complete effect which was important.

There is an echo of such knots in our parks and formal gardens where, as soon as a plant has stopped blooming, it is whisked away and another in full flower is bedded out in its place. We remember them again when we see painstakingly planted and sheared legends and designs made with variously tinted sedums, lobelia and alyssum, in a lawn in front of a public building, or perhaps on a bank by a railway station, announcing the name of a town.

A circular bed crammed with screaming red cannas is another unfortunate survival of a knot garden, and so are files of tulips placed like a pattern of geometrical wallpaper. The current fashion of planting bulbs in drifts is more pleasing to the present taste. Even the derided canna, in pastel shades, placed here and there against a suitable background which shows its immense tropical leaves and its noble clusters of bloom, is coming into its just appreciation.

Although the fashion of Elizabethan knots has passed, they held their own for nearly two hundred years, and doubtless gave Shakespeare much of his prodigious information about flowers, although, oddly enough, he makes no mention of some of the commonest ones, such as snowdrops, forget-me-knots, foxgloves or lilies-of-the-valley, which he must often have seen. However, such omissions are more than balanced by his fleeting and wonderfully vivid descriptions of wild flowers, of trees and shrubs and vines, and his intimate acquaintance with horticulture and rural agriculture in all its departments.

The idea of knots came from Holland, but the parterre came from France.

The parterre was not raised above the level of the ground—hence its name—and it was usually rectangular, the space filled with a scroll-like design, resembling a strip of embroidery. When Le Nôtre was confronted with the problem of what to do with the wide spaces at Versailles, he evolved many intricate designs for such "parterres de broderie." He did not attempt to fill the space with flowers which would not have lived through the winter. Using as models the intricate lacy patterns of jewelers, woodworkers and upholsterers, he planted dwarf box to maintain the design throughout the year. The background was ordinary sand or gravel, while the paths next to the grass were frequently of red sand or colored earth. The embroidery itself was indicated by black earth or iron scalings. There were various ways of making colored earth. Metal was suggested by yellow clay or Flanders tile, powdered; white by chalk, burnt plaster or lime; blue by a mixture of chalk and coal dust; green by camomile.

This incorporation of colored earths into knot gardens was what Sir Francis Bacon referred to in his scornful ". . . they be but toys; you may see as good sights many times in tarts."

There might be borders of flowers around a parterre, and there might be scrollworks of grass in knots. The border might be merely a flat sanded strip, edged on the inner side with box and on the outer with grass and set off by tubs of yew trees or orange trees placed at regular intervals.

Another verdant plaything, costly in time and labor, was the maze. This was an intricate network of paths, hedged by any kind of shrubbery thick enough to keep one from seeing through and high enough to keep one from seeing over. Usually there was a seat or a statue or a fountain in the center, and so cunningly were the paths tangled that often it was necessary to have a high platform overlooking the whole, where a guide might stand to direct those who had become confused and could not find their way back to the entrance.

With gardens planted to suggest mosaics, as in the knots, or crewel embroidery, as in the parterres, living green sculpture was not neglected, and topiary work met this requirement.

This is the clipping, pruning and training of living and growing evergreens into the shapes of urns and animals, birds, grotesque figures, cones, globes and pyramids, and was carried to a high degree of perfection in the early days of Rome, and became fashionable in England during the Elizabethan period. Yew, privet, cypress, box, arborvitae—even holly—were slowly and toilsomely transformed into storks and owls, dogs, children, cupids and musical instruments. Once the metamorphosis was accomplished, it had to be kept at its precise peak of perfection. Otherwise, after a week of rainy weather, you had a squirrel with lavender growing out of its belly and a peacock with a tail at both ends.

The rage for working out these heavily humorous specimens reached a peak in the gardens of Chastleton in Oxfordshire. In the great circular enclosure, laid out in 1720, there grew in living evergreens huge periwigs, vases of flowers and galleons in full sail —best viewed from the windows of the house. Sir Christopher Wren laid out a topiary garden for William III at Hampton Court and, although it no longer exists, there are many descriptions of it. This consisted of nothing less than an entire topiary fort, with bastions, battlements, escarpments and artillery.

Europe was not the only place where such elaborate gardens were fashionable, or where there were clock gardens and water-clocks to mark the passing hours.

In the middle of the eighteenth century Father Castiglione, the Italian Jesuit, was commissioned by the Emperor Ch'ien Lung to design his palace gardens. Father Castiglione introduced horse-shoe stairways, with fifty jets of water spouting from the balustrades, the space between the steps filled by an enormous shell. Below, sitting upright in a circle, were twelve bronze animals in the robes of Buddhist monks. Each beast symbolized an hour, and they followed one another in spouting water for a hundred and twenty consecutive minutes. This led to the Chinese custom of referring to the hour of the dog, the hour of the sheep and the hour of the rat.

More imaginative and certainly more pleasing were those Chinese pleasure grounds where it was not the garden which followed the course of the sun but the spectators who followed a succession of gardens. Thus, this same emperor had one garden with a pavilion where he could watch the peaches ripening, another where he could catch the scent of freshly cut grain.

The garden of Wellington Koo, modern but in the Ming tradition, reveals different scenes not only for every season but for every hour of the day.

Altogether, the most spectacular determination to force flowers to conform with the hands of the clock seems to be found in China.

Dorothy Graham writes with sensitive perception and authority about this in her book *Chinese Gardens*. In it we read that until recently a Board of Mathematicians worked out a calendar each year, which fixed the day for the apricot to bud, and the hour for the millet to be harvested, and so forth. The calendar was submitted to the Son of Heaven for his approval. When this was obtained, on New Year's Day imperial messengers left the

Forbidden City by the Meridian Gate, carrying copies of the ordinance in red sedan chairs on the shoulders of four bearers. Each viceroy of a province received the calendar and he, in turn, informed the people as to the dates. I do not find that the flowers themselves were instructed as to the schedule, and neither do I find what happened if they did not observe it in every detail. Probably it all seemed rational enough at a time when it was believed that the weather could be controlled by Taoist incantations, and a certain note struck on a jade gong could drive away a storm, induce spring breezes and call down dew.

Sometimes the flowers did not receive notice quite so early in the year as to the hour of their blooming and had to make their appearance in a hurry. The Emperor Wu commanded the peonies to open as he passed, and they apparently obeyed.

A thousand years later, in 1900, the old Dowager Empress in Peking had a similar ambition and issued a similar order. We are creditably informed that the gardeners took no chances but slyly inserted charcoal fires in strategic places, so that as the Empress walked past peonies opened like so many prompt little cuckoo clocks.

It is amusing to read of such ingenuities, and to see how, since the days when the Mayas raised their stone almanacs in Guatemala, man has been trying to balance and record the hours of his life against eternity.

Clock gardens are a quaint expression of his attempted measurement of time, and in a sense mazes and knots and topiary work were all clock gardens, for they required an immense amount of time to plant and tend. This was particularly true of the topiary gardens, which might take years to reach maturity. Yew, which was the most popular material, is an extremely slow grower and whoever planted one, with the idea of clipping and training it to resemble a tankard of ale, might be in his grave by the time the green foam poured over the edge.

These elaborate plantings were part of an era when gardeners had unlimited time to labor on the grounds of a great estate, and when the owners had an equal amount of this commodity. People in the country could not travel to London for casual entertainment. They had to find it at home. Puzzling their way through mazes, drinking tea on a terrace overlooking a parterre, strolling around their knot gardens, helped furnish diversions for themselves and their guests.

Perhaps one reason we have grown away from clock gardens may be that modern life is so strictly regimented that we are always conscious of the urgency of time.

Clocks in every room of the house and on our automobile dashboards; watches on our wrists, electric bells in schoolrooms, offices and factories; radio reminders of the exact hour and moment are quite sufficient.

In those all too short periods when we are in our garden we prefer to follow the rhythm of growing, budding, blooming, opening, closing and fading flowers rather than to match them with or force them to follow our divisions and subdivisions of a day, an hour, a minute.

In fact, to keep too sharp an eye on the clock, or even the calendar, destroys much of the pleasure and surprise of a garden. We plant a seed or a bulb or a cutting and go about our business, and in due time we are greeted by a spear of green, by two leaves, by a bud, by a bloom—a miracle as fresh as if it were the first occurrence of the kind in the history of the earth.

Garden time is not a tabulated schedule, but a tranquil and sustaining part of eternity.

The present is now, while we gaze with exquisite delight on the crimped and curdled leaf of the first primrose. The past is what is folded away and dropped with the flowers that have finished their cycle. The future is when we will have a lovelier garden than we have ever had.

Dawn and morning, noon and afternoon, evening and night—these are floral commitments, and no clock or dial or cunningly contrived man-made device can hasten, hold or retard them.

When I am occupied in my garden, I want no timepiece to tell me to hurry or to stop. A happy day is always too short. An unhappy one is always too long. The most ephemeral blossom is a covenant between us and the law that, if we trust to the merciful generosity of nature, our hands and our hearts will reap in appointed fulfillment what they have sown in love.

I saw God in His glory passing near me, and bowed my head in worship.

LINNAEUS

(on the unfolding of a blossom)

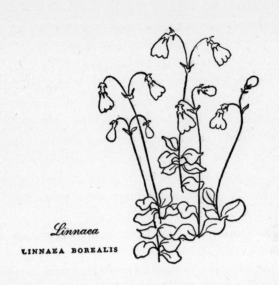

Linnaea

LINNAEA BOREALIS

Over the elastic turf of Lapland there strode in the summer of 1732 a young man whose handsome head was bent forward a little as he searched the vegetation beneath his feet. He did not always stride with buoyant step. He slid down ravines—and nearly lost his life—he pitched around in small boats, he climbed icy mountains, he beat off the gnats which even today make that region a purgatory; he plugged through bogs, he dodged rolling rocks. He was hungry and cold and exhausted, his lungs were elated by the pure air, his mind was joyously occupied with his discoveries, and his heart was filled with wonder at the Creator.

He was five months traversing hundreds of miles of territory which had never been mapped, and he returned home to Upsala with his parcel of a hundred dried plants—hitherto unknown—intact, and his journal neatly written.

According to that journal, Carl Linnaeus—for he was not

yet von Linné—in order to travel with as little incumbrance as possible, was thus equipped for his expedition:

"My clothes consisted of a light coat of Westgothland linsey-woolsey cloth without folds, lined with red shalloon, having small cuffs and collar of shag, leather breeches, a round wig, a green leather cap, and a pair of half boots. I carried a small leather bag, half an ell in length, but somewhat less in breadth, furnished on one side with hooks and eyes so that it could be opened and shut at pleasure. This bag contained one shirt, two pair of false cuffs, two half shirts, an inkstand, pen-case, microscope, and spying glass, a gauze cap to protect me occasionally from the gnats, a comb, my journal, and a parcel of paper stitched together for drying plants." A hanger, a fowling piece, a pocketbook and a passport completed his entire outfit.

Linnaeus was at that time twenty-five years old and in the years which followed—he was to live to be seventy—as in those which had preceded, his passionate and ceaseless study was botany. To be sure, he was also a doctor of medicine in Stockholm; he was a lecturer, a writer and traveler. He was a professor of zoology, mineralogy and biology. He was a husband and father and he was not a little vain of becoming a nobleman with a crest.

But it was the world of plants—the collecting and classifying of them—which gave him that enthusiasm which made him such an attractive figure and such an inspiring teacher.

There are fanciful pictures of him as a tow-headed little boy, gathering plants and wild flowers in the fields and forest and transplanting them into the small garden which his father, the pastor of Rashult, had set aside for him. And there is a charming early nineteenth-century engraving of him as a young man in his small cluttered room. He has just returned from an expedition and has thrown himself, exhausted, into a big carved chair. His legs are thrust straight out in front of him and his head, with long curling blond locks, is resting against the back of the chair. In his left hand is a bunch of flowers he has picked and everywhere are more flowers. They fill a dozen vases, are strewn on the floor, are heaped on top of the oaken, carved armoire and tables, and stuck behind pictures. The botanist is sitting near a table on which lie paper and a quilled pen for making descriptions of his day's gleanings. But his right hand is too exhausted to hold the pen which has dropped from his fingers crosswise upon the paper, and upon it and beside it are more flowers.

The outward life of Linnaeus was not extraordinary. He was a disappointment to his parents because he spent so much time in the fields that first his private tutor at home and then his teachers in grammar school and, finally, the masters in the gymnasium, considered him a blockhead.

Although he was docile enough, he seemed incapable of learning the required theology which was to prepare him for the ministry. Finally, his teachers reported to his humiliated parents that the best course they could advise would be to apprentice him to a tailor or a shoemaker.

Having supported his son at school for twelve years—an expense he could ill afford—his father was pondering what should be done with the so oddly obtuse young man when the provincial doctor made his suggestion. Himself a lecturer in physics, he saw the lad's aptitude and offered to take him into his own house and provide for him for the year he must remain at the gymnasium. Furthermore, he gave him private instruction in physiology and at the same time he directed him along more correct methods of studying botany. Finally (1727), Linnaeus set off for the University of Lund, with forty pounds from his hard-pressed father and a "not very creditable certificate." Here he was to study not theology but medicine.

The years that followed were difficult—the most difficult in a life which was to receive a generous share of friendship, opportunity and honor.

At Lund he lodged in the house of Doctor Stoboeus, professor of medicine, who allowed him free access to his excellent collection of minerals, shells and dried plants, which sent Linnaeus again scouring the fields to collect his own plants and dry them for his own *hortus siccus*.

After a year, he transferred to the University of Upsala, which was the foremost and most ancient in Sweden, and by this time his funds were low indeed. His journal records that "he was obliged to trust to chance for a meal and in the article of dress was reduced to such shifts that he was obliged, when his shoes required mending, to patch them with folded paper instead of sending them to the cobbler."

His tow head was dark brown now, his remarkable eyes brilliant, his every motion quick and light. So attractive was this eager, poverty-stricken youth that when Dr. Olaf Celsius—clergyman and botanist—chanced upon him intently examining some plants in the academical garden, he promptly took him under his wing. He gave him board and lodging in his own house, and the use of his own library which was rich in botanical books.

The worst of the struggle was over. He began to tutor other young men in botany—among them the son of his patron—and to lecture in the botanical garden as an assistant to the aging professor there. He now discovered his gift for teaching and for friendship with youth.

When he was chosen by the Academy of Science at Upsala to visit Lapland as a collector and observer, he left the University without his degree, which he obtained three years later in Holland.

The trip to Holland was made possible by a gift from his fiancée, whose father would not consent to her marriage until Linnaeus had established himself in the practice of medicine.

He spent three and a half years abroad, visiting France and England, and meeting some of the great botanists of the day. He published several books—the *Genera plantarum* being an analysis of all the genera of plants. This and the *Systema naturae*, his *Fundamenta botanica* and *Bibliotheca botanica*, established his fame as a botanist—a fame which gave him the greatest satisfaction.

When he returned to Sweden in 1738, he married and settled in Stockholm, and began the practice of medicine.

He had the not unusual experience of finding that he was more appreciated abroad than at home, and, furthermore, discovered that he "was fonder of meddling with plants than with patients."

It was his good fortune that, at this time, when he was considering leaving Sweden forever, he was elected professor at Upsala. First, he was a professor of anatomy, but was shortly able to exchange this for one of botany, materia medica and natural history.

Now followed the long and happy years when students from his own country and abroad flocked to Upsala to study under him. His knowledge of his subject, his gift for lecturing succinctly and agreeably, infected his pupils with enthusiasm. The number of students at the University had been five hundred. During the lifetime of Linnaeus, it rose to fifteen hundred; after his death it again dropped to five hundred.

During the summer months, twice a week he led the young people—sometimes as many as two hundred—on excursions into the woods and fields. They were divided into parties exploring different areas, and when a rare or hitherto unknown plant was discovered a trumpet was sounded and the whole corps gathered around their teacher to follow his demonstration and listen to his remarks. At nightfall, they came trooping back, their flowers in their hats, marching to the sound of drums and trumpets through the city and to the garden.

Foreigners and persons of distinction from Stockholm journeyed to Upsala to listen to his lectures in classroom or garden
and join in the expeditions to the fields.

The relationship between Linnaeus and his pupils was remarkable. Those petty faults which smudged his nature were consumed in the clear bright flame of his dedication. He was accused
of parsimony, and the days of his extreme poverty may well have
been responsible for this. But with his pupils he was generous indeed. From the poor, and even from some of the rich, the Swedish
lads and the foreign ones, he refused the perquisites for his lectures
to which he was justly entitled. "You are the only Swiss that
visits me," he told one youth, "and I feel pleasure in telling you
all that I know, gratis."

He was fond of money, but he was prouder of his scientific
attainments and proudest of all to inculcate a love of natural history in other minds and hearts.

Inclined to be jealous of other professors and to feud, sometimes violently, with his rivals, with his students he was humble.
"If Fabricus comes to me with an insect or Zoega with a moss," he
wrote in his journal, "I pull off my cap and say, 'Be you my
teachers.'"

Botanical exploration in foreign lands was at that time at-
tended by hazards of many kinds. More than a few of his favorite
pupils, such as Leofling, who was chosen by the Spanish government to travel through their South American possessions, caught
strange diseases and died. And yet there was never a lack of
volunteers for these dangerous journeys and among those who sur-
vived are names well known in the scientific world today.

All through his diary are notes about the achievements of
his pupils, and the many contributions he received from them,
and affectionate personal remarks about their ability, and he constantly marvels at their gratitude. Supersensitive as he was to any
fancied slight or neglect, he found no cause to complain about

hese young people. They followed him willingly and zealously while they were under his direction and held him in reverence after they had gone out into the world and won honor for themselves.

It is pleasant to read of him, after he had grown older, in the diary of one of his pupils who became the celebrated Professor Fabricus. During his college days Fabricus, with two other foreign students, lived in winter directly across from Linnaeus' house. Now, in middle age, the great botanist was growing stout. His forehead was wrinkled and he had a way of walking with his head bent, as if to study the vegetation at his feet. The hair that had been flaxen and then brown was now grizzled, but his eyes were as perceptive and his hearing as acute as in his youth. Clad in his short red house coat, with a green furred cap on his head and a pipe in his hand, almost every day he would drop in at the lodging of the young men, to chat for half an hour which sometimes became a whole hour or even two. He loved to tell them about learned men he had met abroad and he never tired of advising and instructing and encouraging.

In summer, some of these same pupils followed him to his farm at Hammarby and he often came to the cottage where they lodged for six o'clock breakfast. Then he would lecture on the natural orders of plants as long as he pleased, which was usually until about ten o'clock. After that, they would all go into the fields to collect specimens and to discuss their discoveries.

It is pleasant, too, to read further of how, occasionally, the whole family of Linnaeus—his wife and son and four daughters—would come to spend the day with the young men. They would send for a peasant who would play jigs for them on his fiddle and everyone would dance in the farmhouse barn. Sometimes he sat smoking his pipe, delighting in the merriment, and sometimes he would join in a Polish dance in which he excelled them all.

This buoyancy and freshness, this eagerness to learn more

himself and to share his knowledge with others, remained with him until he was stricken with his last illness, and even then, after he was paralyzed on the right side, he cheerfully continued to dictate letters and lectures and notes from his bed, and liked to be carried to his museum to look with pleasure and love upon the treasures he had collected over the long years.

Thus his vivid, magnetic personality, combined with his great learning, made him a legend even during his lifetime, and he enjoyed to the full being received by the Queen, and sought and visited by the great.

Linnaeus died in 1778 and since then his actual contribution to the scientific world has undergone changes in evaluation.

During his life, and for some time afterward, the study of botany consisted chiefly of collecting specimens, discussing and classifying them and pressing or otherwise preserving them. The rank of a botanist was determined by the number of plants he was able to name.

Today, that department of science which deals with the classification of plants and animals is called taxonomy. Other departments have become so extended that many eminent botanists feel they cannot claim to be taxonomists.

Linnaeus put so much emphasis on this particular branch that —necessary as his work was to that which was to follow—it has been argued that it actually retarded inquiry in other fields of investigation. With Linnaeus, biology was, in the first half of the eighteenth century, largely a tedious accumulation of species-naming. The knowledge of the nature of animals and plants, their anatomy, physiology and embryology, was neglected.

Neither is the statement that Linnaeus was the first to recognize the sexuality of plants precisely accurate. It was not the function of the sexual organs which he discovered, but he based his system upon the number, arrangement and fusion of the stamens and their relation to the style.

Upon what, then, does Linnaeus' distinction rest?

It rests, first of all, upon his popularization of the binomial system of nomenclature suggested by another a few years before. Linnaeus, in his *Systema naturae* and other publications, set forth the method of naming every natural production in two words—the first, generic, and the second, specific. He did not originate this system, but he so clarified it that it came into both scientific and common use. All living animals and plants and fossils were hereafter named according to this method, so that men of science in various localities and even in various countries could understand one another and exchange information. For this reason Linnaeus is rightfully considered the founder of nomenclature in natural history and the date 1758 has been accepted as the starting point for determining many generic and specific names. If we, through preference or ignorance, continue to stumble in the floral morass of nicknames, we have only ourselves to blame.

Furthermore, he set the fashion for concise description. Formerly, whole pages were necessary to describe a plant or a flower so that it could be definitely recognized. Linnaeus, omitting verbs and verbiage, worked out a diagnosis of a form including only the essentials he wished to emphasize. "Rosa sylvestris vulgaris flore adorato incarnato" is a terse statement that this is the common rose found in the forests, whose flower is flesh-colored and whose fragrance is sweet.

Finally, he was such a magnificent and inspiring teacher that his pupils became leaders in the natural sciences throughout the world.

He did not seriously construct a natural system of classification. He did, indeed, formulate an artificial system as a convenience for pigeonholing plants then named. The lack of "naturalness" in his system was possibly due to his early belief in the fixity of species.

Fixity of species assumes that at the original stocking of the world one pair of each living organism was created and that all existing organisms are the direct descendants of this pair, without change of form or habit. Linnaeus was such a "special creationist." He believed that there was no such thing as a new species; that any variation was due either to degeneration or hybridization. Later in his life he was to modify this belief, but dominance of the doctrine of special creation prevented him from establishing genuine affinities. His system of classification was artificial, but brought order out of chaos and ultimately gave rise to the ever-changing systems now in use.

The fact that he was a special creationist can be more easily understood if we remember that he was born almost two hundred and fifty years ago, and that to him all nature was, in a literal sense, the handiwork of God Himself.

From his earliest years until his death, he approached his work with reverence and with constant and conscious gratitude to God for making possible such beauty and giving man such delight. As he says simply in his journal, he has "always entertained veneration and admiration for his Creator and endeavored to trace his science to its author." He, who was so dependent upon praise, was always eager to praise God with sincerity and fervor. He was piqued if his colleagues did not bow to his achievements, but he was not ashamed to kneel in rapture before the first brightly flowering furze he had ever seen, when he came upon it on Putney Heath.

It was this pure spirit synchronizing with a clear and untiring mind which makes him unique. One does not have to be a taxonomist; one does not have to be a botanist; one does not even have to be a gardener to feel affection for Linnaeus.

He has been chided because he was vain of the title which was bestowed upon him, but he was modest enough when it came to choosing his favorite flower. This unassuming little plant, with its small, pale, twinlike blossoms faintly streaked with pink, is plentiful enough in Lapland, although it is inconspicuous since it grows in concealing forests. He came across it first on that early Lapland journey and when, later, Gronovius named it *Linnaea borealis,* Linnaeus was delighted. This, together with the magic Lapland drum, he used as a decoration on his coffee cup and saucer which are preserved in the Archaeological and Historical Museum in Stockholm.

Other plants, more showy, Linnaeus named for his friends, and even took revenge on a rival who had criticized him by giving his name to a poisonous plant. But this lowly one was his. Naïvely, he had it incorporated in the crest of which he was so proud.

His personal life had its share of disappointments. The fiancée who had given him her savings so he could travel to Holland and get his degree became a stern and domineering woman whom he regarded with respect and terror. Of his four daughters, two married and two remained with their mother, who lived to a great age. His only son, who inherited some of his father's talents but little of his energy, died in early manhood.

But it was not his worldly success, in which he childishly gloried, or his domestic life, which he accepted philosophically, which made his step so quick and his eyes so beautifully observant. These came from his happiness in the work to which he was drawn when he was a child and which he pursued with undiminished enthusiasm and energy until he was an old man. Fame and financial security were all very well and he put due value—perhaps undue value—upon them. But the natural world, with every object in it formed by the fingers of the Creator—this was his true domain.

When he resigned from his office as Rector of the University of Upsala, he gave his last lecture. Eloquent, clear and moving, it was the statement of his whole life's endeavor and rewards. It was called "On the Delights of Nature."

Love your neighbour, yet pull not down your hedge.

GEORGE HERBERT

Tall oaks, branch-charmed by the earnest stars,
Dream, and so dream all night without a stir.

KEATS

BARE BRANCHES

Seed Pod of Tulip Poplar

LIRIODENDRON TULIPIFERA

The leaves are off the trees, and the beautiful bare skeletons are revealed—the symmetrical branches of the elm and poplar, the white bark of sycamore and birch. Unlike human beings of mature years, who become less attractive as they doff their clothing, these arboreal ladies and gentlemen stand forth in sculptured distinction when stripped of their covering of green summer foliage.

The wisteria and trumpet-vines, which muffle the walls through the summer, now display to full advantage the pattern of their twisted trunks, sketching in sunlight and shadow a design which is strong, yet delicate.

The garden is quiet—no flower colors or forms, only the garden itself with its edging of stone or brick, its stepping-stones, its background of hedge or wall, its accents of evergreens. Now is the time to study and reconsider that allotted space, for we can see its definite pattern and proportions. Form is as fundamental to a well-planned garden as to a well-planned room. If we have covered up basic defects by planting them out, now is the time to correct those errors; to widen or narrow the path, to straighten or curve the edge; to thin out the too-crowded hedge.

Our garden is only a tiny portion of the wide landscape—a panorama that has expanded miraculously since the leaves have gone. The silhouette of mountains or hills, the contour of rolling pasture, the bright course of the brook, the sandy or rocky seashore —all of these, with their pure shadows, are seen with extraordinary clarity. The architecture of the natural world proclaims itself, and there is no veil between us and the stars.

If such grandeur should become too austere, we can come back to the more human aspect of the season. For, with the disappearance of summer's leafy screen, our neighbors' houses become closer and more companionable. We can see the smoke from the hospitable open fires unfurling from their chimneys in the morning, and at night we see their lighted windows. If we are fortunate enough, or wise enough, to like our neighbors, it is pleasant to realize they are within sight—to catch a glimpse of moving figures coming and going.

If we wish to be practical instead of sentimental, this is an excellent time to walk around our own house and study it thoughtfully. For, if a shutter is broken or sagging, if battered trash cans are out of their proper concealment, if the fence has lost a few pickets, we are sharply reminded of our neglect. We can do some pruning of trees and shrubs, too, for it is easy to see just which wayward branches are rubbing together, and just how shapeliness can be obtained or retained.

Nature manages this tremendous alteration of scene calmly. She proceeds with immemorial constancy, to make the shift from verdure to starkness. But although she seems to take her time, we have no time to lose. We must make the most of this brief interval when the leaves have gone but the snow has not yet come. For, with the snow, the distinct outlines from which we should learn our lesson of anatomy become vague. The heavy blanket conceals the path that is too wide or too narrow, the edge that is not straight or not properly curved, hides the broken shutter, minimizes the loss of pickets in the fence. It is even treacherous enough to suggest that a tumbled-down stone wall is rather more pleasing than a mended one, and it piles its white layers cunningly to prove its argument.

No, we shall learn nothing of nature's architecture when the stripped framework has been thickly veneered with snow. There will be another beauty then, but this particular lesson will be obscured.

And we shall learn nothing a little later when the buds begin to swell on every tendril and branch. For with the coming of spring we shall be in no mood to ponder, but shall be rapturously welcoming the first blooms and rolling up our sleeves for the exhilarating horticultural encounter.

Therefore, we must make the most of this brief period, when the trunks and branches of the trees, and the thick stems and fine tendrils of the vines stand forth in that bare beauty which will be clothed in other beauties at other times, but which will remain the basic reason for our esthetic delight.

. . . Everything is fruit to me that thy seasons bring, O Nature. All things come of thee, have their being in thee, and return to thee.

MARCUS AURELIUS

WINTER GARDEN

Dahlia

DAHLIA PINNATA

In those delightful books written about English gardens there are often descriptions of gathering flowers outdoors in January, February and March. There are lists of plants; there are daphne and corylopsis, saxifrages and winter daffodil; there are late wall-flowers and mignonette. There is the Christmas rose. In sheltered spots in Cornwall or Devon the mimosa may be seen in full flower on New Year's Day. Those bright brave buttercups called winter aconite may spread a field of gold above an inch or two of snow. Winter-sweet and winter heliotrope perfume rooms still decked with Christmas holly. Winter heather grows pinker and fresher in the snow. It seems possible to have flowers from your own garden indoors and out during the darkest and coldest months.

Of course, you must select the proper exposure. Of course, you must prepare the proper soil. Of course, you must cut the branches of jessamine and forsythia and witch-hazel, trim off the dead wood and store them in a dark warm cupboard for a week before you bring them into the living room. And, of course, you must have your garden in England.

While the first three injunctions are obligatory, the last is not. There is a surprising number of flowers that will bloom in the United States, even in the most northerly sections, outdoors and in winter. The pasque-flower (*Anemone pulsatilla*) comes up in the snow in North Dakota, and has, quite properly, been chosen for the State flower. In regions south of Washington, D.C., the mume tree is often in full bloom in January. These white and fragrant blossoms last for three or four months, and might be enjoyed by many people who only know them as decorations on Japanese china. Any good garden encyclopedia will list many more winter bloomers, and any good nursery will supply them.

If you have a conservatory—but nowadays who but the very rich include in their architectural plans this adjunct which played such an important part in old-fashioned novels? Opening out of the drawing-room, furnished with red velvet sofas, oriental rugs, dim lights, palms in pots and hanging baskets of geraniums and ivy, it was the stage setting for moments of romance, robbery, and eavesdropping. In it, on occasion, sat ladies and gentlemen in attitudes of fashionable rigidity which simulated attention, listening to expensive musicales.

Even if there were conservatories, the young people of today would not "retire" to them. Their habit is to leave the drawing-room—or more probably the dinette—with no ceremony and, if possible, to leave the house with no delay. Off they go to the nearest movie or night club in winter, and to the swimming pool or beach in summer. The automobile is the accepted scene for romance and robbery, and those occupying it can listen to music or not, by turning a button. A conservatory might harbor an old lady or gentleman, if there are any who acknowledge this title, but probably the present-day oldsters will prefer to join the youngsters.

The conservatory has vanished along with the porte-cochère,

and while most of us on a rainy night regret the latter, the family pussy cat, incurably addicted to fresh scratchable dirt, is the chief mourner for the former.

For those who want to garden through the winter, the small home greenhouse is becoming increasingly popular and practical. This is frankly utilitarian, lacking velvet sofas and oriental rugs, and in it many an amateur learns to raise and handle plants, clippings and flowers with professional skill.

With a greenhouse, a glassed porch or even a bay window, you can have July in January.

All of this presupposes you want July in January.

There are gardeners—even devoted gardeners—who don't.

It may be they are lazy, although the terms gardening and laziness are contradictory. But it may be that the cycle of their own moods and desires synchronizes with the quiescence of those months when nature ceases to surge and swell and bud and bloom, but lies withdrawn in slumber, like Snow White in her crystal cabinet.

A garden that blooms twelve months a year is like a pretty woman who never stops talking. How much prettier she would be if she would, on occasion, emulate the sphinx and let us surmise her thoughts. A living room which is a continuous pageant of flowers picked, bulbs bloomings or sprays forced is like a long concert with no intermission—an endless concert.

This is obviously considered enjoyable entertainment by those people who keep the radio going all the time they are in the house. But there are other people for whom heard melodies are sweet, but those unheard are sweeter, and who turn off the radio at the end of a program.

A gentleman who was a student as well as an indefatigable practitioner in such matters discovered that the heart must pause to breathe and love itself have rest. So who are we to apologize because, after a long summer, we would prefer to abandon the geraniums instead of bringing them into the house to nurse through the winter? We do bring them in and we do keep them alive, but for me it is duty, not joy, that sustains me in the chore.

If you should say aloud that you do not want house plants, you would be regarded as one of those monsters who say they don't like children. All that is meant in the latter case is that you don't like children cutting out paper dolls on your desk, but think it very pleasant to have them in their own quarters. All that is meant in the former is that you don't care for ivy clinging to your living room draperies or rows of glass shelves and potted plants obscuring your view.

In fact, these arrangements may remind you of the Victorian fashion of training ivy to grow around the legs of pianos, and even using the music rack as a sort of elegant trellis.

I have no craving for a little greenhouse to keep the snapdragons blooming a little later or to force the hyacinths a little sooner. Let us all have a vacation from one another, with no hard feelings but only slightly fatigued relief, and meet in the spring to find that our hearts are still as loving and their faces still as bright.

A winter garden whose outline is indicated by a few evergreens and whose surface is a sweep of white snow is not dead. It is gathering and storing its resources for its coming obligations as we, in our withdrawn hours, would do well to gather and store ours.

It used to be fashionable to cover one's walls with so many pictures, hanging brocades, painted plates, niches for statuary and brackets for ornaments that the decorations overlapped like scales on a fish. The eloquence of vacant spaces has only recently been recognized.

This eloquence may be repeated in gardens and in the single bouquet of evergreens or dried leaves and grasses in muted tones.

In Sweden, on Midsummer Eve, Maypoles bound with fresh

birch boughs and decorated with wreaths are raised in every town. Around these whirl dancers, leaping, stamping, clapping. The red and black aprons from Rättvik, the heavily embroidered petticoats from Floda, the dainty kerchiefs of Leksand intermingle with the yellow buckskin breeches, scarlet tassels, flowered waistcoats and wide-brimmed hats of their partners. The men and women, the boys and girls, have practiced these folk dances all winter in barns and sheds and out in the fields, and now they rush together in a vigorous pageant—swaying, bowing and jigging—from midnight until morning.

In the same way their flower gardens, which have barely six weeks to speak their entire piece, are crammed to bursting with every conceivable meeting of pansies and pinks, daisies and dahlias, columbines and chrysanthemums. It is all very gay—the midsummer dance of the men and women, boys and girls—the midsummer revel of the whole calendar of flowers. Very gay and very brief.

In our gardens, which may last four months, for eight and even longer according to climate, there is no need of pushing and crowding, and we can sit out a dance or two if we choose. There is space, even amid the flowers which are blooming, for those which are resting or preparing to appear.

There is space and time for a winter garden from which the last lingering mignonette has gone and in which the first primrose has not arrived.

All artists know—or learn—that in music, in sculpture, in painting, in poetry, in architecture, there is a rhythm which rises and falls; which repeats itself; which sinks into a whisper. Upon such rhythm depend unity, grace and reserve. Such rhythm is in nature. Such rhythm may be in a garden. It moves in varying intensities in the far north where the winters seem to last forever and in the far south where it is always summer. But it is there, and recognition of it is a special art.

I was pondering this one winter evening.

Outside, the snow lay quiet and deep and the moonlight glittered on icicles hanging from the trees. Vibrations were hushed. There was no color in the white expanse—only shadows of varying darkness.

Inside, the room was quiet, too. The Siamese cats had poured their sculptured length upon the floor before a fire that breathed almost as softly as they. My book lay open but I was not reading.

As I thought of my garden, motionless under the snow, I felt as a mother must feel when all the children are safely tucked in their beds, unstirring, making no demands. In the morning they will wake with calls and laughter, shouts and endless motion, and with them will come pleasures and duties, labor and recompense. But just now, for a few hours, they are asleep and the mother may without guilt give herself to other thoughts and other pursuits.

Yes, that is the way it is with a garden. I need not even think about it tonight. I need not plan what shrubs are to be transplanted, what trees to be pruned, what clumps of perennials to thin, what vines to train, what fall bulbs to plant, what spring ones to separate.

No, I will be quiet, as the Siamese cats are quiet, as the winter garden is quiet. I have a long evening to read whatever I choose.

I close my book and put out my hand for another. It came this very morning and with the first sentence I am lost to everything else. Gradually, as I turn the pages, my excitement mounts. Now I am far away from the tranquil room. I read absorbedly, avidly, and a hundred visions chase themselves through my imagination.

My book is a new garden catalogue.

Friend, walk thine own dear garden grounds,
Not envying others' larger bounds;
For well thou know'st 'tis not extent
Makes happiness, but sweet content.

HERRICK

THE GARDENS OF THE HESPERIDES

Pansy

VIOLA TRICOLOR HORTENSIS

Where the Gardens of the Hesperides were no one precisely knows. They bloomed in the antiquity of time on the borders of the western ocean where the sun sets. In them lived the Hesperides sisters—three beautiful girls or maybe four or maybe seven. They were the daughters of Cerberus and Night, or maybe of Atlas and Hesperis. In any case they had delightful voices and sang as sweetly and as unweariedly as the Sirens.

Although we cannot place the Gardens of the Hesperides in any exact geographical location, we understand that they produced a remarkable fruit which was nothing less than apples of gold. These grew on a tree guarded by a dragon and in some legends there is only one apple and this is the sun itself. But there must have been more, for it is positively stated that Heracles, directed by the nymphs, found the garden, slew the dragon and carried the apples to Argos and afterward to Athena. Another crop were the proper gifts at the marriages of Cadmus and Harmonia and Peleus and Thetis, since they were symbols of fruitfulness. Furthermore, the golden apples which Aphrodite gave to Hippomenes before his race with Atalanta came from the same trees.

These gardens, whose name is so musical and whose fruits were so obviously unpalatable, and whose occupants were so indefinite as to number and parentage, have bloomed in the literature of mankind since the age of mythology.

They are the gardens of the imagination, and as such are forever immune to frost and hail, snow and winds and every killing curse. They bloom afresh and perennially with each succeeding human generation. Being intangible, they partake of eternity.

Actually they are not far away in either time or space. The garden you yourself plan and tend and love is the garden of the Hesperides. It glitters in the sunshine and shimmers in the rain. You can see it clearly when you wake in the darkness of night or when you lie in sleep upon your bed. It is as brilliant in winter as in summer. It is exquisitely balanced and patterned and most charmingly blended in color, tint and tone. Every plant is perfect. There is not a weed. It is the dearest garden in the world. It is your garden.

Not this year, of course. Next year.

BIBLIOGRAPHY

A complete bibliography of books about gardening would fill many hundreds of pages. This is merely a list of some of those which are referred to in the text.

AN ISLAND GARDEN. Thaxter, Celia. Houghton Mifflin & Co., Boston, 1895.

ART OF PERFUMERY. Piesse, George William S. Piesse and Lubin, London, 1891.

CARNIVOROUS PLANTS. Prior, Sophia. Field Museum of Natural History, Chicago, 1939.

CHINESE GARDENS. Graham, Dorothy. Dodd, Mead & Co., New York, 1938.

FLOWERS AND FLOWER LORE. Friend, Rev. Hilderic. Nims & Knight, Troy, N. Y., 1889.

FRAGRANCE IN THE GARDEN. Dorrance, Anne. Doubleday Doran, Garden City, 1937.

GARDENS AND HOMES OF MEXICO. O'Neal, Cora M. B. Upshaw Co., Dallas, Texas, 1945.

ITALIAN PLEASURE GARDENS. Nichols, Rose S. Dodd, Mead & Co., New York, 1928. Also 1931.

NATURAL HISTORY OF THE BIBLE. Tristram, H. B. Society for Promoting Christian Knowledge, London, 1868.

ORCHID HUNTERS (THE). MacDonald, Norman. Farrar and Rinehart, Inc., New York, 1939.

OUR FLOWERING WORLD. Platt, Rutherford. Dodd, Mead & Co., New York, 1947.

Plant Lore and Garden Craft of Shakespeare (The). Ellacomb, Rev. Henry N. W. Satchell & Co., London, 1884.

Plants of the Bible. Moldenke, H. N. and A. L. Chronica Botanica Company, Waltham, Mass., 1948.

Practical Encyclopedia of Gardening in Dictionary Form. Edited by Norman Taylor. Halcyon House, Garden City, N. Y., 1942.

Story of Biology (The). Lacy, William A. Garden City Publishing Company, Garden City, N. Y., 1925.

This Green World. Platt, Rutherford. Dodd, Mead & Co., New York, 1947.

Thomas Jefferson's Flower Garden at Monticello. Betts, E. M. and Perkins, H. B. The Dietz Press, Richmond, Va., 1941.

Thomas Jefferson's Garden Book. Annotated by Edwin Morris Betts. The American Philosophical Society, Philadelphia, 1944.

The World Was My Garden. Fairchild, David. Charles Scribner's Sons, New York, 1938.

Your Garden in the City. Gomez, Natalie. Oxford University Press, New York, 1941.

INDEX

INDEX